Di[illegible] to Reco[illegible]ry of Adrenal Fatigue Syndrome

An Introduction

Michael Lam, M.D., M.P.H.
Dorine Lam, R.D., M.S., M.P.H.

Diagnosis to Recovery of Adrenal Fatigue Syndrome: An Introduction
by Michael Lam, M.D., M.P.H. and Dorine Lam, R.D., M.S., M.P.H.

Published in the United States by:

Adrenal Institute Press, Loma Linda, CA 92354
www.AdrenalInstitute.org

Cover and Interior Design: Nick Zelinger, NZ Graphics
Editing: John Maling (Editing By John), Virginia McCullough
Book Shepherding: Judith Briles

ISBN (paperback): 978-1-937930-23-3
ISBN (ebook): 978-1-937930-24-0
Library of Congress Control Number: 2012943713

Diagnosis to Recovery of Adrenal Fatigue Syndrome: An Introduction
Michael Lam, Dorine Lam. First edition, 2012

10 9 8 7 6 5 4 3 2 1

1. Health 2. Adrenal glands—Disease. 3. Fatigue 4. Stress (Physiology) 5. Neuroendocrine

First Edition

Printed in the United States of America

Contents

Author's Note

The most common AFS symptoms patients report to their doctors include: lack of energy, lethargy, dizziness, insomnia, hypoglycemia, low blood pressure, and anxiety. In determining AFS status, a thorough history must be taken by an astute and experienced clinician—the evaluation is far superior to laboratory tests.

- Routine diagnostic tests used as part of the workup for fatigue and a low energy state are normally negative.
- In each stage of Adrenal Fatigue Syndrome, crash and recovery takes on different characteristics, durations, and intensities.
- Most adrenal crashes, even in advanced states, can be managed with the right tools and approach.

When Adrenal Fatigue Syndrome has entered your life, especially in the advanced stages, it is normal to experience crashes

Diagnosis, managing crashes and crafting your recovery are key components in any Adrenal Fatigue Syndrome healing and revival program. To be effective, each component must be personalized to one's unique inborn constitution. *Diagnosis to Recovery of Adrenal Fatigue Syndrome: An Introduction* will go in depth into each of these areas and will provide the missing links in answering the questions that traditional medicine has missed.

Dr. Lam

Note: This book is part of Dr. Lam's Adrenal Recovery Series™ and all information can be found in *Adrenal Fatigue Syndrome: Reclaim Your Energy and Vitality with Clinically Proven Natural Programs.*

Introduction

Fatigue and lethargy are two of the most common complaints doctors hear from their adult patients, both of which are symptoms of a silent epidemic condition known as Adrenal Fatigue Syndrome (AFS). This condition is as old as humankind, but its incidence has skyrocketed as our society and our lifestyles have become increasingly complex and high-pressured.

From a sufferer's point of view, Adrenal Fatigue Syndrome is confusing and frustrating. We can see the everyday consequences of Adrenal Fatigue Syndrome in the following statements:

- I'm tired all the time—I manage to keep going on my job, but I drink coffee every few hours to get through
- I used to merely gripe and complain about feeling tired, but now the fatigue is so overwhelming and debilitating, I'm underperforming on my job.
- I'm anxious and fearful much of the time.
- I seem to catch every cold or flu that comes around.
- My joints ache, and my doctor said I probably have arthritis, even though I just turned 40.
- I'm depressed and can't think straight—I feel like I walk around with brain fog.
- I've tried every diet in the book, but I can't lose weight.
- I wake up at 3:00 AM and toss and turn for hours and cannot fall asleep again.
- I used to have great energy, but now a short walk wears me out.

These statements personalize some of the typical—and persistent—signs and symptoms of Adrenal Fatigue Syndrome. You might have described these same things to your doctor, or you may have noted these changes in your health or know someone who has these complaints, but you don't know what to make of them. If you're over age forty-five or fifty, you might even be told to attribute your symptoms to "normal" aging!

Below, you'll find an expanded list of the signs and symptoms of Adrenal Fatigue Syndrome. Not surprisingly, many of these symptoms are also related to other conditions, and they match the statements listed above:

- Often feels tired between 9:00 and 10:00 PM, but resists going to bed
- Difficulty getting out of bed in the morning
- Cravings for salty, fatty, and high protein food such as meat and cheese
- For women, increased symptoms of PMS and irregular menstrual bleeding, with days of heavy flow that stops (or nearly stops) on day 4, only to resume on days 5 or 6 of the menstrual cycle
- Pain in the upper back or neck with no apparent reason
- Tendency to feel better on vacation and when stress is relieved
- Food and or inhalant (air borne) allergies
- Dry and thin skin
- Hypoglycemia but blood sugar is normal
- Low body temperature despite thyroid medication

- Heart palpitations when heart is normal
- Unexplained hair loss
- Recurrent miscarriages in the first trimester
- Low blood pressure, dizziness, and vertigo

As you can see, Adrenal Fatigue Syndrome has a broad spectrum of symptoms, many of which seem nonspecific, and, therefore, are often reframed as psychological in origin, such as anxiety or depression. Sometimes patients are told that these symptoms are "nothing that some rest won't cure." However, it is clear that Adrenal Fatigue Syndrome is not that simple. Research shows that AFS at its core represents the body's neuroendocrine stress response when under threat.

Do not confuse AFS with Addison's disease.

Addison's disease is often caused by an autoimmune dysfunction, whereas stress and a host of other factors are the primary culprits of Adrenal Fatigue Syndrome. The symptoms of Addison's disease include low energy, joint and abdominal pain, weight loss, diarrhea, fever, and electrolyte imbalances. Some AFS sufferers report these symptoms too, but they are usually much less intense.

Both lead to low cortisol output in the adrenal glands, though those with AFS can be symptomatic despite the fact that laboratory tests are usually normal. Currently, conventional medicine recognizes only Addison's disease as a legitimate disease of low adrenal function. If, for example, you ask your doctor if your symptoms could point to Adrenal Fatigue Syndrome, you may learn that he or she has not heard of AFS or may deny its existence.

Adrenal Fatigue Syndrome (AFS) consists of four broad and overlapping clinical stages, from mild to severe. Stages 1 (Alarm

Reaction) and 2 (Resistance Response) are generally mild. Some fatigue is present, but not debilitating. Few are alerted and seek professional help. By the time Stage 3 (Adrenal Exhaustion) arrives, most have seen their physician for lack of energy and are usually told all is well after an extensive workup. Fatigue in Stage 4 (Adrenal Failure) is severe and most sufferers are bedridden.

Prologue

If you are seeking information found in this book, then it's likely that you or a loved one has experienced symptoms or changes in your health status that you can't explain. Perhaps the symptoms or changes came on slowly over time. For example, you don't feel quite as energetic as you once did, and you can't figure out why. Until recently you maintained your weight with a balanced diet and a couple of walks or bike rides or trips to the health club each week. You seldom complained about insomnia or fitful sleep, but now you can't seem to get a good night's sleep. You've told your doctor that you've been feeling down and tired and now you have to force yourself to get through the day.

Today's physicians commonly hear these kinds of statements. In fact, fatigue and anxiety are two of the most common complaints doctors hear from their adult patients, both of which are symptoms of a silent epidemic condition known as Adrenal Fatigue Syndrome (AFS). This condition is as old as humankind, but its incidence has skyrocketed as our society and our lifestyles have become increasingly complex and high pressured.

The Many Symptoms of Adrenal Fatigue Syndrome

From a sufferer's point of view, Adrenal Fatigue Syndrome is confusing and frustrating. It's difficult to grasp that so many symptoms, often associated with a host of other conditions, could point to AFS. We can see the everyday consequences of Adrenal Fatigue Syndrome in the following statements:

- I'm tired all the time—I manage to keep going on my job, but I drink coffee every few hours to get through the day.

- I used to merely gripe and complain about feeling tired, but now the fatigue is so overwhelming and debilitating, I'm underperforming on my job.
- I'm anxious and fearful much of the time.
- I seem to catch every cold or flu that comes around.
- My joints ache, and my doctor said I probably have arthritis, even though I just turned forty.
- I'm depressed and can't think straight—I feel like I walk around with brain fog.
- I've tried every diet in the book, but I can't lose weight.
- Last year I lost my job, and shortly after those emotional and financial blows, I've been chronically tired and depressed.
- I wake up at 3:00 AM and toss and turn for hours and cannot fall asleep again.
- I used to have great energy, but now a short walk wears me out.

These statements personalize some of the typical—and persistent—signs and symptoms of Adrenal Fatigue Syndrome, most likely Stage 3 (discussed later). You might have described these same things to your doctor, or you may have noted these changes in your health or know someone who has these complaints, but you don't know what to make of them. If you're over age forty-five or fifty, you might even be told to attribute your symptoms to "normal" aging!

Below, you'll find an expanded list of the signs and symptoms of Adrenal Fatigue Syndrome. As you can see, many of these symptoms are also related to other conditions, and they match the statements listed above:

- Progressively increasing lethargy and lack of energy
- Increased effort needed just to perform daily tasks
- Decreased ability to handle stress
- Tendency to gain weight, coupled with an inability to lose it, especially settling around the waist
- Frequent bouts of influenza and other respiratory diseases, with symptoms lasting longer than usual
- Trembling under pressure
- Reduced sex drive
- Tendency to feel lightheaded especially when rising from a horizontal position
- Inability to remember things
- Lack of energy in the morning and in the afternoon between 3:00 and 5:00 PM
- Tendency to feel better suddenly for a brief period after a meal
- Often feels tired between 9:00 and 10:00 PM, but resists going to bed
- Difficulty getting out of bed in the morning
- Once out of bed, needs coffee or other stimulants to get going
- Cravings for salty, fatty, and high protein food such as meat and cheese

- For women, increased symptoms of PMS and irregular menstrual bleeding, with days of heavy flow that stops (or nearly stops) on day 4, only to resume on days 5 or 6 of the menstrual cycle
- Pain in the upper back or neck with no apparent reason
- Tendency to feel better on vacation and when stress is relieved
- Mild depression
- Food and or inhalant (air borne) allergies
- Dry and thin skin
- Hypoglycemia
- Low body temperature
- Nervousness
- Heart palpitations
- Unexplained hair loss
- Alternating constipation and diarrhea
- Dyspepsia (indigestion)

As you can see, Adrenal Fatigue Syndrome has a broad spectrum of symptoms, many of which seem nonspecific, and, therefore, are often reframed as psychological in origin, such as anxiety or depression. Sometimes patients are told that these symptoms are "nothing that some rest won't cure." However, it is clear that Adrenal Fatigue Syndrome is not that simple.

As you will learn, this condition from a scientific perspective represents the body's normal neuroendocrine stress response when under threat. (Neuroendocrinology is the study of the extensive interactions between the nervous system and the endocrine system.)

Chapter 1

Diagnostic Tests—What You Need to Know

Developments in modern medicine allow us a wide array of laboratory tests designed to help diagnose certain disease states, along with measuring the severity of the disease and the burden on the body. We have literally thousands of tests available to us, but your doctors must choose the correct ones to evaluate whether you have Adrenal Fatigue Syndrome, and they must understand the limitations of these tests.

Routine Laboratory Tests for Fatigue

The most common AFS symptoms patients report to their doctors include: lack of energy, lethargy, dizziness, insomnia, hypoglycemia, low blood pressure, and anxiety. In an otherwise healthy person, conventional medicine workups to investigate these symptoms include:

- Hematology, a complete blood count (CBC) to detect or rule out anemia which measures red cells, white cells, and platelets.
- Biochemistry to rule out systemic organ damage such as liver and kidney disease.
- Inflammation in the blood through the ESR, *erythrocyte sedimentation rate*,and *C reactive protein*, both markers for inflammation.

- Cancer markers for early detection of cancer.
- Blood sugar levels to rule out diabetes mellitus and glucose intolerance.
- Urine testing to rule out infection or kidney damage.
- Fecal occult blood to rule out bleeding from the gut and to screen for cancer.
- Electrolyte panel to assess kidney function.
- Thyroid stimulating hormone, T4, and T3 levels to rule out thyroid malfunction.

These tests can detect *macroscopic* pathology such as major organ failure in the form of diabetes, heart disease, metabolic dysfunction, cancer, liver failure, kidney failure, and thyroid diseases. Unfortunately, these routine tests do not detect organ dysfunction at the subclinical level, such as those afflicted with subclinical hypothyroidism, Adrenal Fatigue Syndrome, mild liver dysfunction, subclinical imbalanced electrolyte function, minor hormonal imbalances, and suboptimal detoxification capacity. In addition, many conventional physicians pay little if any attention to laboratory values that lie close to or just outside of normal range, both at the low- or high-normal levels.

We also have a wide array of standardized testing protocols. These protocols are well intentioned in that they are meant to efficiently detect most common medical problems with both accuracy and speed. However if patients' results fall within the statistical norm, regardless of symptoms, the patient is often considered normal even though they suffer from unpleasant symptoms. Conventional medicine testing is limited in these cases. Saying that nothing is wrong often leads patients to embark on various kinds of programs on their own.

Complex conditions like Adrenal Fatigue Syndrome, subclinical hypothyroidism, chronic fatigue syndrome and tension myositis syndrome are difficult to evaluate precisely because routine laboratory values usually fall into the standard normal range. Even when laboratory tests indicate abnormalities, many doctors are unable to correlate these clinical findings if the patient's symptoms, often referred to as "presentation," are confusing or convoluted, as we often see with AFS. It's no wonder patients are frustrated when they feel tired and lethargic, among other symptoms, but they are deemed well.

Before we had super-sophisticated testing, physicians relied primarily on detailed histories and physical examinations. Laboratory values were used to confirm a diagnosis or clear up doubt.

Sadly, thorough examinations and taking detailed histories are fast becoming lost arts. The results are alarming because ill people are sent home after being told the laboratory says they are well. This is why so many patients struggle alone, going from one specialist to another. Often feeling abandoned, they fall into despair.

When Normal is *Not* Normal

Considering the sophistication of modern medicine, most find it hard to believe that a person with symptoms of AFS could end up with normal laboratory test results. Consider the following:

- Most AFS sufferers have low immune function, so they have frequent infections. However, a blood test shows a normal white cell count. What is poorly understood or ignored is that normal or low normal white cell counts can be a sign of poor immune function. As well, nutritional deficiencies, such as low zinc, magnesium, B vitamins, and essential fatty acids can contribute to poor immune functions, so a normal white cell count does not rule out these problems at the subclinical level.

- Normal platelet count does not rule out stealth viruses or a residual bacterial infection, such as that seen in post-acute Epstein-Barr (EBV) virus infection. This is a member of the herpes virus family and one of the most common human viruses. Low or low normal platelet count can be a sign of toxic stress from viral causes or emotional forces.
- A normal fasting blood sugar in absolute terms, but with symptoms of clinical hypoglycemia present, is common in advanced stages of AFS.
- Normal electrolyte levels do not rule out the presence of debilitating subclinical dilutional hyponatremia as seen in advanced Adrenal Fatigue Syndrome.
- A normal TSH, free T3, and free T4 do not rule out secondary subclinical hypothyroidism associated with adrenal and neuroendocrine dysfunction. Similarly, a normal TSH can be present in those with clinical hypothyroidism. In other words, you can be suffering from primary hypothyroidism clinically but have normal TSH levels. *In fact, current conventional medicine protocol calls for starting a patient on thyroid medication based on significant symptoms alone even if TSH is normal.*

- We often see normal blood aldosterone and sodium levels accompanied by salt craving and low blood pressure in sufferers of advanced AFS.
- Normal potassium levels do not rule out the need to reduce the internal potassium load. In Adrenal Fatigue Syndrome, sodium depletion is common, leading to a relative (and not absolute) potassium overload that when tested is still within normal laboratory range.
- High normal liver enzymes usually suggest liver dysfunction, typically from chemicals such as medications or resulting from poor nutritional status. Normal liver enzymes are commonly associated with suboptimal clearance of metabolites in AFS as the body slows down to conserve energy.
- High normal or high total cholesterol could mean low levels of vitamin D and is commonly associated with hypothyroidism.

Many chronic illnesses, including AFS, progress over time slowly. Relying solely on routine blood serum laboratory tests for a definitive assessment is an extremely incomplete approach.

Functional Laboratory Testing

Functional and specialized laboratory testing go beyond standard testing and offer a window of insight into the way our bodies are working. These tests generally focus on the endocrine, gastrointestinal, immunology, and metabolic systems, along with the nutritional function of the body.

Some of the most popular specialized tests, but not necessarily what is needed in most cases, include:

- *Organic acids urinary analysis* to assess the efficiency of cellular energy production and metabolic toxicity.
- *Neurotransmitter assessments* to determine serotonin, dopamine, GABA, and epinephrine/norepinephrine levels.
- *Digestive stool analysis* to gain information about intestinal absorption, intestinal metabolism, enzyme level markers, stool pH, detection of pathogenic microorganisms, levels of beneficial bacteria, fecal color and occult blood, and gut immune function via IgA levels.
- Small intestine bacterial overgrowth breath test *for assessment of bloating, gas, diarrhea, and irregular abdominal pain.*
- *Intestinal permeability analysis for assessing leaky gut, irritable bowl, and malabsorption syndromes.*
- *Liver detoxification tests,* including various challenge tests to evaluate the detoxification pathway and capacity.
- *Immunoglobulin testing* to evaluate the classical immediate reaction (IgE allergy) to pollen, or the delayed reaction (IgG allergy) results from poor digestion and leaky gut syndrome. Both are prevalent in AFS and environmental illnesses. These tests can also be helpful to assess toxic reactions from residual infections such as that caused by Epstein-Barr virus and Candida.

Other potentially helpful tests include:

- *Lyme disease testing,* because this can mimic AFS.

- ATP/cellular energy tests to assess mitochondrial function (the energy producing structures in the cells).
- Bone resorption assessment to identify early bone loss.
- Melatonin profile for assessment of circadian pattern and seasonal affective disorder (SAD).
- Amino acid analysis to assess chronic fatigue, depression, and immune problems.
- Essential and metabolic fatty acids analysis to assess inflammatory reactions.
- Urine iodine with pre- and post-loading tests to identify iodine/iodide sufficiency.
- Helicobacter pylori specific antigen (HpSA) stool tests to determine if the stomach and duodenum contain H. pylori, which is a major cause of peptic ulcers.

As you can see, the list is long, and one can become overwhelmed. However, as with other tests, each functional test offers a narrow peek into the inner workings of the body from a specific perspective, but is seldom definitively diagnostic. Normal values do not rule out pathology, and abnormal values require clinical correlation to make sense.

With modern technology there is a tendency to over-test. If we perform enough tests, it is almost impossible not to find some small abnormality. However, that doesn't mean that each abnormality needs to be acted on. In fact, some abnormalities may not pose a health threat at all, but the unnecessary treatment can actually hurt you.

Some of the most common overused tests include whole body scans, virtual colonoscopies, and high tech mammography.

Treating the Numbers

We often see a rush to treat patients based on abnormal lab values rather than through the whole person approach. We can call this "medicine by the numbers." It's a common clinical approach, but as with regular blood tests, reference ranges for functional testing are not perfect. In addition, tremendous statistical variation exists. What is applicable to a general population group may not be applicable to any given individual. Patients need astute, open minded clinicians to know what tests to order and how to correlate the laboratory findings with the clinical history in order to make sense of these test results.

Experienced clinicians know what to look for, along with the pros and cons of each test. However, *patients* must be aware of the pros and cons of clinical tests, too. As an example, the following tests are frequently ordered but are seldom necessary for assessment of Adrenal Fatigue Syndrome, for reasons outlined:

- *Serum (blood) magnesium:* This test doesn't tell us about the magnesium where it counts—inside the cell. To really look at magnesium closely, an intracellular magnesium level test should be ordered.

- *Total T4 and total T3 (for thyroid function):* This test doesn't tell us what counts. A *free* T3 and *free* T4 are required.

- *Serum (blood) essential fatty acids:* Deficiencies are nearly universal, so we don't need to measure them.

- *Serum (blood) vitamins A, C, and E:* Since deficiencies are widespread, we don't need a test to confirm them.
- *Vitamin B profile, including thiamin (B1), riboflavin (B2), niacin (B3), vitamin B6, folic acid, vitamin B12:* Deficiencies are pandemic, so we don't need to test.
- *Serum test for estrogen and progesterone:* Doesn't tell us the free levels present, which is what is important.

Laboratory Tests Specific to Adrenal Fatigue Syndrome

As we've said, AFS is difficult to evaluate with traditional blood tests. Those available are designed to detect the severe, absolute deficiencies of adrenal hormones that characterize Addison's disease. Blood testing is also useful to detect extreme, excessive levels of adrenal hormones associated with Cushing's disease. In other words, available blood tests measure adrenal hormones only at the extremes.

For a minute, picture a bell curve. The ACTH (adrenocorticotropic hormone) challenge test is the standard acceptable test for definitive diagnosis of Addison's disease. It reveals extreme underproduction of adrenal cortisol output, as shown by the bottom few percent of the bell curve. This means adrenal function must be extremely low in order to fit a recognized diagnosis. However, symptoms of non-Addison's adrenal weakness and low cortisol output can begin to appear after a moderate deviation from the mean on the bell curve. Therefore, the adrenal glands could be functioning well below the norm and not be detected by the ACTH test.

What this tells us is that a test result showing so-called *normal* levels of adrenal hormones does not mean that one is free from adrenal malfunction at the subclinical level. As long as one is not on alert for AFS, these blood tests lead to misguided interpretations. Many tested for adrenal function are told the results are well within the *normal* range, but in reality, their adrenal glands are performing suboptimally; meanwhile, clear signs and symptoms continue as the body cries out for help and attention.

Serum (blood) and *urine* laboratory studies are commonly used. Unfortunately, they cannot be relied upon for accurate diagnosis. They can indicate AFS indirectly. For example, a morning serum cortisol level of under 15 mcg/dL (normal range 5-23 mcg/dL), or a mid-afternoon level of under 10 mg/dL (normal range 3-16 mg/dL) may serve as warning of sign of underlying AFS when accompanied with symptoms of fatigue. A 24 hour urine cortisol with results in the lower 1/3 of normal reference range also serves as alert of AFS. It should be remembered that most AFS sufferers have normal serum and urine cortisol levels.

Serum tests of two surrogate markers of adrenal function, cortisol and DHEA (measured in the blood by way of DHEA-S) and their ratio can tell us if the body is in an anabolic state (build up) or catabolic state (breakdown). However, these blood levels alone do not provide clear evidence of AFS.

Saliva testing: We can test adrenal health by measuring levels of key adrenal hormones such as cortisol, progesterone, estrogen, testosterone and DHEA in the saliva. A saliva test is more accurate than blood tests to measure free and circulating amounts of both cortisol and DHEA, as opposed to the total amount, which is what is measured in the blood.

We can measure DHEA at any time during the day, but cortisol levels vary throughout the day. Generally they're at their highest in the morning and lowest in the evening before bedtime. For this reason, the recommended tests require four saliva samples taken at 8:00 AM, 12:00 PM, 5:00 PM, and before bedtime.

Multiple saliva samples give us the ability to map the daily curve of free cortisol in the body relative to DHEA levels, allowing us to have a much clearer picture of adrenal function. The following are general correlations on how saliva cortisol and DHEA levels relate to Adrenal Fatigue Syndrome:

- Normal cortisol, normal DHEA does not rule out AFS.
- Normal cortisol, high DHEA points to early stages of AFS or excessive DHEA intake.
- High cortisol, normal DHEA points to early AFS as the body puts out more cortisol relative to DHEA as part of the stress response.
- High cortisol, low DHEA usually points to early phases of Stage 3 AFS.
- Low cortisol, low DHEA usually is associated with late phases of Adrenal Exhaustion.

The above correlations are very general, and we see many exceptions to the rule. It gives you a general idea that proper interpretation is much more than simply looking at the absolute numbers on a laboratory report. In addition, paradoxical values are common, especially in those who have a sensitive body or are in advanced AFS. Delayed response needs to be factored in as well.

How to Properly Interpret Saliva Cortisol Test

Saliva cortisol test has many limitations. Results can be confusing and oftentimes defy conventional medical logic. To be useful, saliva cortisol levels must be viewed in the proper context. Keep in mind the following:

- Morning free cortisol level is indicative of peak cortisol output modulated by the HPA axis.
- Lunch cortisol level points more toward cortisol adaptability.
- Mid-afternoon cortisol is highly associated with metabolic issues such as blood sugar imbalances.
- Evening cortisol level refers to baseline adrenal cortisol function. As AFS advances, the daily cortisol diurnal curve changes, as shown in Figure 11.

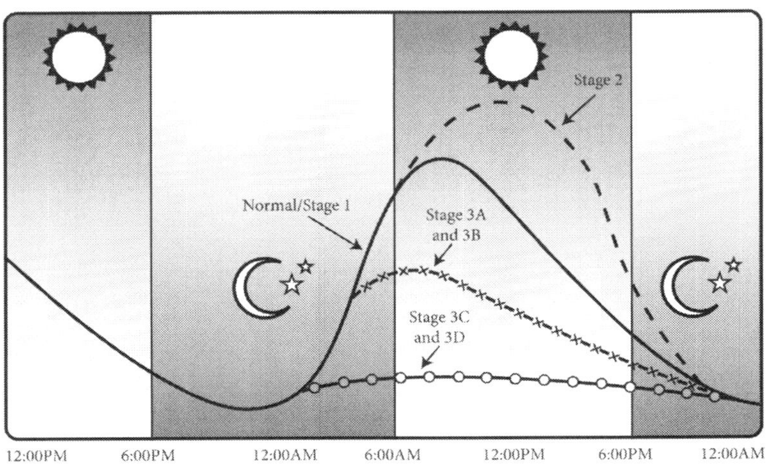

Figure 11. AFS Stages and Circadian Release Of Cortisol

Those in Stage 2 generally see a rise in total cortisol output, especially in the morning which can linger well into the afternoon as the adrenal cortex is put on overdrive. Those in early phases of Stage 3 will see morning cortisol declining from a high level back to normal, and then as Stage 3 progresses, the morning cortisol level becomes low. Most in Stage 3C or later experience flat cortisol output throughout the day. The 24 hour cortisol curve is flat, as shown above.

Many exceptions exist to the above generalizations, so we can't rely totally on a test result to make clinical decisions. For example, some who are in Stage 2 show high evening cortisol but low or normal morning cortisol. These individuals tend to have low energy in the morning but are alert as evening arrives. Then, despite high evening cortisol, they often sleep well and don't have sleep onset insomnia that commonly plagues those with elevated evening cortisol. Even after a night's rest, though, they tend to be sluggish in the morning. Others may show both high noon and nighttime cortisol levels, with normal morning and afternoon levels. This may be reflective of the body's erratic response to increase cortisol output during the day when faced with episodic stressor events.

For reasons not well understood, some clinically in Stage 3 may exhibit Stage 2 Adrenal Fatigue Syndrome cortisol curve pattern. A small number of people can have a totally normal cortisol curve while in late phases of Stage 3. This should alert us to further investigate whether other conditions are the ultimate root cause. It should be clear that proper clinical correlation is critical. Few test results are straightforward. Over reliance on cortisol values alone as a yardstick of adrenal function can therefore be misleading.

Another pitfall is that it is easy to stay overly focused on cortisol as the main culprit of AFS. This is a common mistake. One doesn't need to have a statistically abnormal saliva cortisol curve to have AFS. In fact, some healthy people have abnormal cortisol curves, and not every abnormal cortisol curve exhibits itself as Adrenal Fatigue Syndrome. Those who are preoccupied with bringing the cortisol level back to normal as the main goal of recovery invariably fail.

Remember that AFS is a complex condition with many causes. In advance stages, the entire neuroendocrine system is dysregulated. Low cortisol is but one of many parameters to consider. As mentioned earlier, a small number of sufferers in advanced stages of AFS can present with totally normal twenty-four hour cortisol patterns, but yet they clinically present with all the classic symptoms. Saliva test as an absolute diagnostic tool for AFS leaves much to be desired and is far from perfect.

In addition, be wary of computerized laboratory interpretations, as they have limited value. In fact, it can be misleading if we fail to match the different cortisol values with the body's symptoms throughout the day along with the clinical state.

Note: If you are taking oral hormones or applying topical supplemental hormone creams such as DHEA, steroid, insulin, or pregnenolone, the saliva or blood test results may be elevated. False elevation can also occur if the test is done within 90 minutes of exercise, in times of unusual stress, within 6 hours of caffeine intake, or

within a few hours after a physical injury. It is best to avoid taking hormone supplements well before testing. Those who are on prescription medications are particularly vulnerable to inaccurate test results. Drugs such as oral contraceptives, thyroid medications, pain medications, SSRIs, benzodiazepines for anxiety, statins for lipid control, and anti-epileptics can lead to a flattened 24 hour cortisol curve due to blunting of cortisol release.

Stress is another factor to consider at the time of testing. Cortisol levels tested after a quiet and relaxing morning may be different from those taken when you are under tremendous stress.

Warning: Cortisol and other hormonal levels vary widely among individuals; in addition, the body is in a constantly changing state. Because of these variables you should agree to undergo these laboratory tests only with professional guidance and the reassurance that these tests are both relevant and cost effective. Not to be forgotten is the fact that not all laboratories are of the same quality as well.

As you know by now, Adrenal Fatigue Syndrome symptoms can be numerous and severe while at the same time, laboratory results are normal. The reverse is also true. The test results could show abnormal levels of cortisol and DHEA, but one might not be experiencing symptoms. Furthermore, in advanced Adrenal Fatigue Syndrome, the twenty-four hour saliva cortisol curve invariably becomes flattened most of the time and can stay that way for an extended period, even during recovery. Sometimes we see a delayed response, which means the test results may be confusing and misleading and show no meaningful change while symptoms are improving.

Suffice it to say, overreliance on tests is a common adrenal recovery mistake.

Saliva testing is best used in serial studies performed only as needed for comparative purposes. Relying on a single hormonal snapshot to draw clinical conclusions is another common mistake in recovery. This is especially common among those who are not under professional guidance. For example, patients may rely on laboratory tests without understanding their limitations. They then embark on a self guided nutritional recovery program that eventually leads to improper use of nutrients, thus making the condition worse. Again, a thorough history taken by an astute and experienced clinician is superior to lab tests and is the most accurate way to assess AFS status. If you are not sure if you have AFS, need a baseline picture, or if you are not recovering from AFS, the saliva cortisol test can be very helpful, provided that it is always properly interpreted by an experienced and qualified health professional who knows your history.

Key Points to Remember

- Routine diagnostic tests as part of the workup for fatigue and a low energy state are normally negative.
- Normal test results may indicate underlying abnormal function, but this is often overlooked.
- Functional laboratory testing can be helpful, but most are not needed.
- Many are treated based on numbers and test results, especially those with abnormal laboratory thyroid function results. Some are given thyroid replacement medication based on symptoms alone.
- Laboratory tests specific for Adrenal Fatigue Syndrome also are not conclusive and, to be of value, require proper interpretation.
- Saliva cortisol tests, in particular, are often misinterpreted.
- Single saliva tests are often misleading as the results vary widely among individuals.
- Saliva testing is best used in serial studies and only as needed by a practitioner who knows what to look for.
- In determining AFS status, a thorough history taken by an astute and experienced clinician is far superior to laboratory tests.

Chapter 2

Typical Adrenal Fatigue Syndrome and Crash Progression

By the time most women and men come to us for help, they are already in advanced stages of Adrenal Fatigue Syndrome. Many are surprised at the extent of damage done to their bodies, but few are surprised if we ask them to take a step back and do a detailed personal life history. Over the years, we've found that only a minority of sufferers developed Adrenal Fatigue Syndrome due to acute stressful events, such as accident, surgery, infection, and emotional traumas. Most have had signs and symptoms of AFS for many years and even decades, but have ignored them for far too long. Acute events merely serve as triggers of adrenal crashes more often than not.

A typical picture emerges, and you need to understand this. It's really quite simple: Your body behaves logically. Any history, while not 100 percent predictive of the future, often indicates what is likely to happen ahead. A thorough knowledge of AFS progression will help you anticipate and prepare for what may be coming ahead. Now that you understand the physiology behind AFS, especially the crashes, we think you will find this discussion vital.

We often reiterate that in Stages 1 and 2, most people experience symptoms, including fatigue, but recover quickly and never realize that Adrenal Fatigue Syndrome was a factor. In fact, except in the cases of extreme stress and rapid onset of Adrenal Exhaustion, most patients realize they have experienced many crashes and recoveries along the way to Stage 3 and its phases. A crash in Stage 1 is hardly noticeable, while a crash in Stage 3C will invariably land you in bed for days. Not all crashes are the same. Here, we examine more closely the nature of these crashes in each stage (previously described in this book).

The following diagram shows the typical general progression of Adrenal Fatigue Syndrome over time, with steady deterioration during the generally asymptomatic Stages 1 and 2. This is followed by a rapid and functional decline in Stage 3, which is especially severe in Stage 3C. If unattended, the natural progression is likely to end in adrenal failure. Note that the exact progression varies from person to person with wide variations in intensity and timing. Furthermore, multiple crashes usually occur along the way, and the entire progression typically lasts a decade or more.

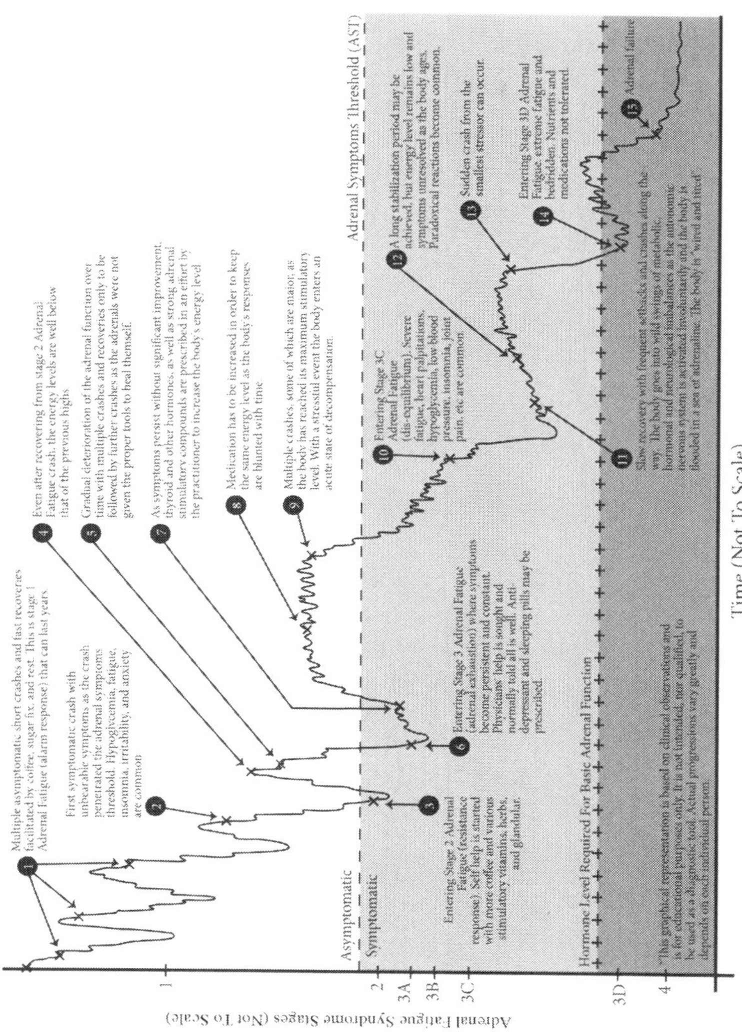

Figure 14. Typical Adrenal Fatigue Syndrome Progression

Stage 1 Adrenal Fatigue Syndrome (Alarm Reaction, points 1-3 on the chart, previous page)

In this stage, the body is alarmed by stressors and mounts an aggressive anti-stress response to reduce stress levels. Brain norepinephrine is activated and the mind is put on alert. Unfortunately, this subclinical state is seldom recognized as a pathological condition. Blood sugar levels become imbalanced, resulting in low energy and usually remedied with quick fixes, such as soda drinks, energy potions, and high carbohydrate foods such as pastries and other sweets. Those who require coffee to start the day may already be in this stage but are unaware of it. If a major crash occurs, recovery usually takes a few days or weeks at most and full recovery is achieved. Crashes in this stage usually go unnoticed and are only evident in retrospect.

Stage 2 Adrenal Fatigue Syndrome (Resistance Response, points 3-5)

With chronic or severe stress, the adrenals eventually become unable to compensate. Those in this stage still carry out normal daily functions, but the sense of fatigue is pronounced at the end of each day as the body needs more rest than usual to recover. Despite a full night's rest, the person often doesn't feel refreshed in the morning. Anxiety and irritability begin to set in. Insomnia becomes more common, as it takes longer to fall asleep, and waking in the night several times is common. Infections become more recurrent. PMS and menstrual irregularities surface, and symptoms suggestive of hypothyroidism (such as a sensation of feeling cold and a sluggish metabolism) become prevalent. Those who require multiple cups of coffee to sustain them throughout the day may well be entrenched in this stage without knowing it.

Compared to Stage 1, the frequency of minor and major adrenal crashes is higher. The intensity is also increased. The Adrenal Symptoms Threshold (AST) has been penetrated on the downside. A mild degree of adrenal symptoms are usually present before the crash, but not always. During the adrenal crash, these symptoms worsen and may be exaggerated, but they're still manageable.

At this stage, many individuals recover fully with no symptoms after the crash as they rise above the AST, but not all are so fortunate. A significant number of people remain symptomatic below the AST after recovery. They might manifest symptoms that are slightly worse than the state they were in before the crash. These crashes are often what bring sufferers to their physicians for the first time. Medical workups are usually normal.

Crashes associated with Stage 2 Adrenal Fatigue Syndrome are characterized by a higher intensity of symptoms compared to crashes associated with Stage 1. To start, the pre-crash energy level is lower than Stage 1 Adrenal Fatigue Syndrome at the baseline. At the height of the crash, the adrenal function usually descends and penetrates the AST. Debilitating symptoms start to appear, including anxiety, insomnia, and low blood sugar. As with crashes associated with Stage 1 AFS, each crash and recovery cycle end at an adrenal function status that is slightly compromised. This is a gentle downward cascade of functions resembling a waterfall or a series of steps going down. The duration of the recovery phase is usually longer when compared to that experienced in Stage 1.

Stage 3A Adrenal Fatigue Syndrome (Early System Dysfunction, points 6-9)

As the body enters Adrenal Exhaustion (Stage 3), the clinical picture drastically worsens. Mild symptoms characteristic of Stages

1 and 2 Adrenal Fatigue Syndrome continue to worsen and become clinically evident. Symptoms become persistent or chronic, including any of the following:

- The slightly elevated blood pressure now becomes low throughout the day.
- Mild musculoskeletal pain turns into chronic myalgia around the clock.
- Frequent recurrent infections are the norm in comparison to intermittent infections.
- Occasional mental feeling of blues becomes mild depression.
- Sleep patterns become more disrupted as insomnia becomes chronic.
- Fatigue that usually occurs during the end of occasional stressful days becomes an everyday event.

We see the ability to carry out normal daily activities moderately reduced. Most people are exhausted after a full day's work. However, not all organs are dysfunctional to the same degree at the same time. The organ system that is constitutionally weakest is the first one to decompensate, while another organ system appears to be intact. The HPA axis dysregulation is responsible for many of these symptoms.

Minor crashes become increasingly common, occurring once every few weeks. Major crashes usually occur farther apart. Symptoms are prevalent pre-crash, and because most are longstanding, most sufferers have adapted to them, although they live at a lower energy baseline level. During the adrenal crash, the symptoms worsen. Even after recovery, the body remains symptomatic, and below the AST most of the time.

Stage 3B Adrenal Fatigue Syndrome (Hormonal Axis Imbalances, points 9-10)

The endocrine system in our body is linked hormonally in a series of axes for optimal function. Dysfunction in one system invariably affects the others, leading to a cascade of decompensation as the body weakens. In this phase, hormonal axes such as the ovarian-adrenal-thyroid (OAT) axis in women and adrenal-thyroid (AT) axis in men are particularly compromised.

When these axes become imbalanced, the adverse feedback loop creates a vicious cycle of cascading decompensation involving multiple organ systems at the same time. In women, this could typically involve symptoms associated with low thyroid, progesterone, and cortisol hormones. In the male, the adrenal-thyroid axis may be compromised. Sufferers' physical and emotional states continue to deteriorate and they enter into a state of confusion. By that we mean they are unable to logically dissect the myriad systemic manifestations of multiple hormonal axes imbalances.

Compared to those experiences in Stage 3A Adrenal Fatigue Syndrome, crashes are usually more intense and more frequent as the adrenal reserve is depleted. It is not uncommon to have minor crashes every few weeks, and major adrenal crashes every few months. The body never fully recovers to a point that the energy is consistently above the AST at any point in the crash and recovery cycle.

Stage 3C Adrenal Fatigue Syndrome (Disequilibrium State, points 10-13)

The body gathers steam as it continues its downward path of impaired functions. Gradually, the body becomes severely compromised in trying to maintain the fine controls of homeostasis.

Therefore, normal equilibrium is lost. The body will try its hardest to maintain equilibrium. The autonomic nervous system (ANS) is now put into overdrive as a way to overcome perceived danger and impending doom. The body is flooded in a sea of norepinephrine and epinephrine. However, the compensatory response systems can become dysregulated. Along with damaged receptor sites, impaired metabolic and detoxification pathways exist in what is now a low clearance state, leading to paradoxical and exaggerated responses.

Clinical manifestations include swings in blood sugar levels, with reactive hypoglycemia being the hallmark, along with fragile and low blood pressure, postural hypotension, and the inability to remain standing for a prolonged period of time. Reactive sympathoadrenal responses include heart palpitations, night sweats, and reactively driven anxiety followed by depression. Normal activities are usually very much restricted.

Crashes that occur in this phase are fast and furious. Minor adrenal crashes can occur every few days, and major ones are not far behind. There is a roller coaster ride of ever worsening symptoms. It is not unusual for one to go from a minor crash immediately into a major crash before the minor crash has even completed its recovery. A state of constant fatigue exists, with severe energy depletion. The highest rate of functional decline occurs at this phase. A major crash can be very scary and may require trips to the emergency room. The recovery phase for Stage 3C crashes can be many more times longer than that of Stage 1.

Stage 3D Adrenal Fatigue Syndrome (Near Failure, points 14-15)

As the body's various hormones, such as cortisol and aldosterone, fall below the minimum required reserve for basic normal function, the body continues to down regulate the amount needed in order to preserve what is on hand for only the most essential body functions. This down regulation further reduces cortisol output, exaggerating a vicious downward cycle. The body may not be able to tolerate steroids, or the response may be blunted. Even at low doses, normal nutrients are often systemically rejected by the body. Unstable hormonal positive feedback loops are activated which invariably worsen the condition.

Those who are in this stage often live in the hopeless state of constant crashes. The body is too drained to mount a productive response. Adrenal crash symptoms are usually extreme. Minor crashes can be intermingled with major crashes. Emergency room visits are common due to unstable blood pressure, irregular heart rate, and severe anxiety with a sense of impending doom. Sufferers are usually bedridden and require help to carry out daily self care and minimal chores.

In addition to a much longer recovery time compared to Stage 3C, sufferers remain symptomatic well below the AST throughout almost the entire crash and the recovery experience. Those in late Adrenal Exhaustion have a very low adrenal pre-crash reserve at baseline. Compared to earlier stages, stress triggers can be something that would not have triggered a crash in early stages. This may be a longer than usual walk or inadequate fluid intake. The body is much more sensitive to stressors as adrenal weakness progresses.

Fortunately, most adrenal crashes, even in advanced states, can be managed with the right tools and approach (discussed later in Part II). In the next chapter, we get a glimpse of what happened in the life of one woman when Adrenal Fatigue Syndrome advanced into Adrenal Exhaustion and remained unrecognized and untreated for many years.

Key Points to Remember

- The typical Adrenal Fatigue Syndrome sufferer goes through multiple crashes and recovery cycles over decades as the body slowly decompensates.
- In each stage of Adrenal Fatigue Syndrome, crash and recovery takes on different characteristics, durations, and intensities.
- Precipitating events often act as major triggers for each crash.
- Most AFS sufferers can look back at their history and see a progression of symptoms.
- Generally speaking, as AFS progresses, crashes become more frequent and more intense. The trigger needed to precipitate a crash reduces. Recovery also becomes less strong and takes longer as AFS advances.

Chapter 3

Mary's Story—Illustrating the Problem

The narrative that follows is a mini-case history of a woman named Mary, but her story matches that of millions of women. We've included it because in Mary's story, we see a woman pass through early stages of Adrenal Fatigue Syndrome and through Adrenal Exhaustion to near failure. The numbered graph included at the end of this chapter will help you follow along and see the progression of Adrenal Fatigue Syndrome in one typical sufferer.

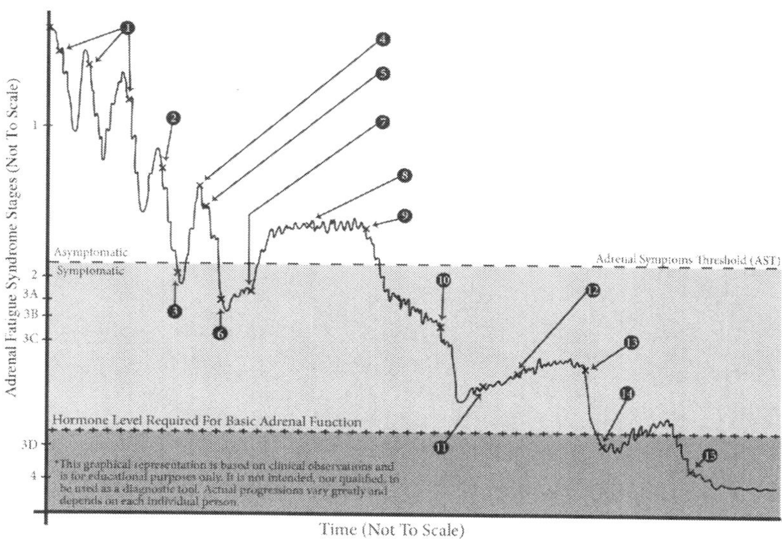

Figure 15. Typical Adrenal Fatigue Syndrome Progression
(See Figure 14 for notes in Figure on each point in progression. They are absent in Figure 15 but explained in the text.)

Mary's adult life started much like many normal teenager's after a healthy childhood. As with many young people, Mary began to test—and stretch—the limits of her body around the time she went off to college. For the first time in her life, Mary independently arranged her own schedule and social life. Wanting to embrace everything in her new life, she stayed up late studying and socializing with her new friends and exploring the exciting city where her college was located, while also working as a waitress a few hours a week.

When she first noted feeling tired in the morning and dragging through her day, she revved herself up with coffee drinks and sweets to keep going until the weekend when she could sleep in until noon. (Point 1 in the diagram.) By Monday, she would feel fine again. Since her roommate and other friends lived the same way, Mary saw nothing unusual about her college lifestyle.

During these young adult years, her menstrual period occasionally was a little slow in coming, and she noted with frustration her stubborn premenstrual acne, but here, too, she saw nothing out of the ordinary. As long as Mary could stay up late, but still manage the extra fatigue, she believed everything was normal.

Mary had no idea she was already in Stage 1 of AFS Syndrome, and even early Stage 2.

Approaching her senior year in college, her family experienced some financial problems, which meant they could no longer help out with her school expenses. Mary increased her student loans and found a second part-time job. Throughout that year, she felt especially pressured to strike out on her own and find a job soon after graduation.

During her senior year, a friend noted that Mary seemed stressed out and suggested that running would help her cope. Once she started running, Mary enjoyed challenging herself and pushed past the fatigue she felt after a mile or two. She didn't think there was anything unusual about being so tired at the end of each run. Rather, she believed she had let herself become out of shape, and therefore, continued to treat her fatigue with coffee and quick energy sugary foods. On a few occasions she was so tired after a run that she was forced to take a nap, but neither she nor her friends considered her extra fatigue unusual. (Point 2)

At this point, Mary was in an environment that was, in a sense, self-reinforcing. Other students lived much the same way, and Mary herself saw that many of her friends faced challenges far more daunting and intense than her own. Older professors and Mary's parents would not have seen anything of note in Mary's student lifestyle. However, Mary lived with Stage 1 AFS, experiencing small crashes from which she quickly recovered. It would never have occurred to her to call these episodes adrenal crashes.

After Mary graduated, she returned home. She took a waitressing job while she did an extended job search, which took almost six months. Finally, she found an entry level corporate job in a suburb not far from her hometown. She launched into an independent life and was determined to do well as she climbed the corporate ladder. Mary brushed off the periodic crashes and minor fatigue that began to be part of her daily life. Being young and strong and ready to embrace life, she pushed through the week, relying on snacks and coffee. Sometimes she'd overeat at lunch and feel mentally foggy through the afternoon—a sign of a food coma. Like others in her office, she drank coffee or tea and ate chocolate to help her stay awake during late-afternoon meetings. She also had energy drinks with her so she could keep her energy up and found an herbal formula at a health food store to fend off fatigue. (Point 3)

Always in the back of Mary's mind were her family's financial problems, which eventually forced her parents to move from the family home to a small apartment. The first year on her job, Mary used her vacation days to help with the move, which wore her out. Again, here, she was experiencing the crashes of Stage 1, but for the most part, her body bounced back. Later, with each recovery, however, she felt less well and never fully renewed, despite periods of rest. (Point 4)

Her father had developed heart disease, which worried Mary and her siblings, and motivated Mary to stay physically fit, even entering races. She was disturbed that she could barely finish a 10K road race, but she was too busy to give it much attention. Around this time, Mary found herself taking over-the-counter pain medication to ease her menstrual cramps, she also developed benign lumps (fibrocystic changes) in her breasts, which made her breasts tender and painful during the week or ten days prior to her premenstrual period. When she asked her doctor about these symptoms and her irregular periods, she was told that these were not serious—many women experience the same cluster of menstrual complaints.

Here we see Mary developing *estrogen dominance.* We also see what happens when symptoms that are *common* are confused with being just a *normal* part of being a woman.

Mary's doctor gave her a standard answer but failed to link these signs of estrogen dominance to potential health problems down the road. True enough, millions of women develop these symptoms and they are considered by many a normal part of women's menstrual cycles. When something is considered normal, that usually means it isn't taken seriously and is rarely linked with the big picture of health or declining health. Mary continued to try to catch up on sleep during her weekends, much as she had in college, but she never quite came back as strong as she had before. These adrenal crashes were taking a toll, but her body still had reserves.

As is common, Mary remained in Stage 1 and early Stage 2 throughout her twenties and early thirties, but nothing seemed particularly unusual about her symptoms. Plus, she was always grateful each time she bounced back from bouts of fatigue and mental exhaustion. Like so many people who lead hectic lives, Mary brushed off her intermittent symptoms as the normal peaks and valleys of modern life. She read magazine articles about women who were determined to get ahead and have it all, and while that described her, she tried to take care of herself and avoid the pitfalls of this strenuous life journey.

Mary advanced in her career, eventually being hired by another company at a higher salary and a more impressive title. She married and was soon pregnant with her first child. As much as she wanted children, she confided in friends that she found pregnancy quite stressful, especially when she had to go away on a couple of business trips during her second trimester. Although she continued to manage, her overall energy level continued to drop. (Point 5)

Mary continued working until a couple of weeks before delivering her baby and returned to her job a few months later. Two years later, she had her second child, and admitted to her husband that she was relieved to have their two healthy children, but certainly wouldn't have more. Her childbearing years were over.

The two pregnancies changed Mary's hormonal patterns, and although only in her late thirties, she began complaining to her friends about putting on extra pounds, pointing out, too, that her skin was especially dry. Like many women in Mary's generation, she felt anxious about both her family and her job. When she was home, she thought about work, and when she was at work, she thought about home. She resented her husband's lack of willingness to do his fair share of childrearing or the chores necessary to keep their home going. Eventually, this resentment and other difficulties whittled away at their relationship, but Mary put on a united, happy front to family and friends. She only confided to one close friend about her dissatisfaction with her married life.

When her father died suddenly, Mary unsuccessfully attempted to keep going through her continuing exhaustion (Point 6), but her grief was so deep that she sought counseling to help her cope. Meanwhile, her menstrual difficulties continued, and she experienced symptoms like brain fog and fitful sleep. Mary understood that her life was stressful, but she didn't have information to connect her symptoms to Adrenal Fatigue Syndrome.

At forty, Mary had crossed the threshold from Stages 1 and 2 of AFS and into Stage 3, Adrenal Exhaustion. She had symptoms all the time, meaning that she no longer snapped back from bouts of fatigue; sleep didn't renew her energy, as it had during her college years and during her twenties and into her thirties. She always found reasons for her symptoms, though, so she could tell herself that soon the stressful times would ease. Unfortunately, her life took twists and turns over the next years, including a nasty divorce, the source of ongoing stress.

Although she no longer ran, Mary walked to maintain her fitness level and to keep extra pounds off. She also spoke with her doctor about the array of symptoms that were her daily companions—anxiety and constant mild depression, and fatigue that never completely went away. Her doctor eventually ordered various tests, including thyroid function, but the results fell into the so-called normal range. Still, Mary's doctor believed that she was suffering symptoms of a stressful life and prescribed antidepressants and sleeping pills, which became hallmarks of life in her forties. (Point 7)

Being highly intelligent, Mary read about stress and its effects on health, and she embarked on a self-guided journey to get a handle on her life. Despite disappointments in her personal life, she was proud of her professional accomplishments. However, she felt anxious about continuing her progress and had a nagging sense that the unrelenting pressures at work had taken a toll.

Like many women approaching midlife, she tried to reassess, but fatigue itself sometimes prevented her from fully taking stock. In addition, as a single parent, she had a tremendous amount on her plate. Mary began to rely on nutritional supplements, and she tried various herbal formulations guaranteed to boost energy. In fact, she became an avid consumer of health information and natural food store "cures." When these OTC remedies, plus antidepressants, seemed to work, Mary again felt optimistic and believed she'd turned a corner toward well-being. (Point 8)

Mary's happiness, unfortunately, did not last. While her health and energy levels stabilized for a while, she needed more supplements to sustain the same energy level. This worked for a while. One day, she received news that her best friend had died in a car accident. This was a major stressful event (Point 9), and Mary's symptoms came crashing back—literally. Fatigue returned, even worse than before, along with thinning hair and continued dry skin. Supplements seemed to be less effective than before. She also had many food cravings and steadily added pounds. Mary's doctor ordered more thyroid tests and added a synthetic thyroid hormone replacement to an already long list of medications. Again, she seemed to improve a bit, and friends encouraged her to get back to the gym and join a weight loss program to shed the extra pounds. Mary continued to have regular minor crashes that went on for a few years. Her body gradually weakened over time as fatigue became more prominent with each crash.

By this time, Mary had fallen deep into Stage 3C (Point 10), and she struggled to keep up with her job and children and turn her life around. By her mid-forties, even she realized that she was living a marginal life, barely hanging on. Almost all her non-work hours were spent recovering her strength, which meant she seldom saw friends and used all her energy to keep up with her children's activities.

Odd and new symptoms appeared as Mary's chronic symptoms steadily worsened. She developed allergies and sensitivities to fluorescent light, and she was on edge and anxious most of the time, even startling when her phone rang. In addition, she took periodic courses of steroid medications to treat bouts of bursitis, and she also suffered constant muscle and joint pain.

Adrenal crashes became more frequent, with longer, slower recovery periods. As she approached menopause, Mary felt hopeless and disappointed in her efforts to improve her health. Her periods were irregular and heavy, and her doctor warned that a hysterectomy was in her future, as uterine fibroids had developed and were growing in size. This was another sign of estrogen dominance, but her doctor was not familiar with that connection. With increasing fatigue, she had to take time off from work to get more rest, and her body slowly recovered. (Point 11)

Mary lived—uncomfortably—in Stage 3C for many years. During this time (Point 12), she began experiencing paradoxical reactions to medications and nutritional supplements. Tired all the time, she also felt wired when she took vitamins and adrenal glandular recommended by a nutritionist. Instead of helping her, she felt odd and what she called wired-and-tired. (Point 13) Eventually, Mary's efforts to cope with the symptoms and still function, even marginally, gave way when a major crash hit that landed her in Stage 3D. (Point 14)

Looking back to her college years, if anyone had told Mary that she'd need to take an extended medical leave of absence from her job, she wouldn't have believed it. However, even Mary's psychiatrist recommended this step, explaining that depression and stress had weakened her. As a precaution, Mary's doctor again tested her adrenal function to rule out Addison's disease, but again, the results fell into the normal range. Because she felt lightheaded and experienced blood sugar drops and surges, Mary was tested for diabetes, and was considered pre-diabetic, though her serum fasting glucose was invariably normal. Her frequent hypoglycemia was clinically confusing. Finally, she was told that conventional medicine could do no more for her.

Mary decided to use her medical leave to work hard at getting well. This started with a detoxification program she'd read about; she even tried coffee enemas. She tried, again, to meditate and she sought spiritual direction, but she couldn't shake the mental fog and confusion that dominated her days. The detoxification plan backfired, intensifying the symptoms and sending Mary to bed rest days at a time.

This time was also marked by numerous trips to the ER with heart palpitations, extreme dizziness, and weakness. These symptoms reminded Mary of her father and his premature death. On each trip to the ER, she was told that it was likely she'd had a panic attack or had eaten something that produced allergic symptoms.

Going back to work was out of the question, and by this time Mary was already living off the proceeds of the sale of her house. Her midlife years turned out to be nothing like she'd expected.

At this point, Mary was incapacitated, and in addition, she felt very much alone. (Point 14) Mary had turned into a patient for whom no diagnosis quite fit and no treatment worked over an extended period of time. By the time she found an integrative doctor, Mary couldn't tolerate most of her medications, including even the low dose of hydrocortisone meant to help correct her symptoms which were consistent with low cortisol seen in AFS. Her new doctor eventually gave up.

Having little other choice, Mary spent the better part of three months in bed. She gradually regained some strength, although she experienced periodic crashes throughout her recovery and she was always at risk for crashes. She now took a basket of more than ten different nutritional supplements every day with little effect. She spent hours online visiting various forums on fatigue and trying out different modalities as suggested by fellow sufferers. The harder she tried, the worse she became. She finally realized that her damaged body needed personalized attention and guidance as she was at the end of her road. Further trial and error was only making her worse. In her early fifties by this time, Mary had many signs of aging, from dry, wrinkled skin to thinning bones and arthritis. Most of all, she realized that she felt old and tired, and also sad that, starting in her late thirties, she'd begun missing out on the joy of life.

How Mary Recovered

Every day, countless individuals like Mary are in desperate search of a way to regain their life and vitality. Mary was fortunate because her body, though severely damaged, managed to recover with time and a proper recovery program.

Eventually, Mary was able to return to work close to her home. By this time, Mary had reconnected to what mattered most to her.

She no longer felt the need to strive and get ahead. She felt a sense of calm and peace as she returned to a lifestyle that matched her body's capacities and ability to handle stress in a creative fashion. She built a life rich in quality, which is a blissful place to be. Mary emerged from the long nightmare, regretting the time she lost feeling tired and unhappy, but grateful for her life and the recovery she achieved. She also hoped that her example would influence her children's lives and inspire them to find greater balance.

The key to Mary's story was her persistence. She took responsibility for her health and her care. After multiple false starts that stretched over years, Mary finally found a nutritional program through the *Dr.Lam.com* web site. Mary's story is meant to inform, not alarm, but it provides the kind of narrative that reflects the path many walk. Of course, many women and men will continue to pursue active lives and big goals. Our hope is that with the knowledge of Adrenal Fatigue Syndrome, adults will live more thoughtfully and pay attention to the symptoms of stress and adjust their lives accordingly.

Mary's story describes the problem, a summary of sorts of a typical long term progression of AFS. It pulls together, in the story of one person, the information you have read thus far. In the next section, we discuss the kinds of things Mary did to gain a good degree of recovery and find balance in her life.

Key Points to Remember

- Mary typifies many women and men who ignore the signs of AFS for too long while they pursue their careers, raise families, and try to manage hectic schedules that simply can't be sustained.
- Mary's symptoms are typical of someone who advances through the various stages of Adrenal Fatigue Syndrome.
- Fortunately, Mary took corrective action with the right professional in the nick of time and recovered well.

Chapter 4

The Adrenal Crash and Recovery Cycle

Adrenal crashes are very common and almost every person with Adrenal Fatigue Syndrome has experienced them. We define adrenal crash as *a state of acute adrenal weakness.* The body's compensatory mechanism to stress has been overwhelmed. To ensure survival, the body initiates a series of actions designed to conserve energy. An adrenal crash represents such an effort by the body as it down regulates and returns us to the most basic form of survival—a vegetative state.

Crashes are usually characterized by severe fatigue, and, in extreme cases, incapacitation.

Many individuals in Stages 1 and 2 of Adrenal Fatigue Syndrome have experienced adrenal crashes, but they often are not aware of it. They may be aware of incidents or periods of stress and fatigue, perhaps with loss of stamina and disturbed sleep. But these symptoms pass as the body recovers. These early stages of AFS can last for years and even decades before progressing to the later stages.

However, as AFS progresses, the crashes become more frequent and severe, ultimately, in many cases, moving into Stage 3 phases. As symptoms increase, many people report them to their doctors, at which point, they are often diagnosed as individual health problems, such as hypothyroidism, PMS, or depression. The adrenals are seldom identified as the potential source of the symptoms.

The First Alarm Bells Ring

Crashes are usually the first alarm bells to ring early on in Adrenal Fatigue Syndrome. However, more to the point, those who have never heard of AFS are also familiar with crashes. Given the general attitudes about cycles of fatigue, these crashes can appear completely harmless, even normal, which helps explain why Stage 1 and even Stage 2 can go on for years or decades.

For example, many people expect to have short periods of extreme fatigue or exhaustion, which spontaneously improve immediately after taking a nap or resorting to a sugar fix. In fact, in our society, a sugar fix has long been considered a normal response to a midmorning or mid-afternoon slump, which we can liken to a minor crash. Drinking a great deal of coffee can bring on a caffeine crash after the stimulating effect of caffeine has worn off. Overwork, excessive exercise, crowded schedules, and so forth can bring on fatigue, which is often viewed as a normal part of life. Many individuals often say aloud that all they need are "a few days off," or, "a good night's sleep," or "the emergency crisis at work to end."

With time, however, these crashes become more frequent and intense. As AFS becomes more severe, perhaps progressing into Stage 3, a crash can be triggered by something as simple as taking a longer than usual walk, and it can last for weeks and even months in extreme cases. Of course, these crashes can vary greatly in intensity, depending on the stage of Adrenal Fatigue Syndrome.

With each crash, the body usually recovers on its own, or the individual perceives that things are back to normal. However, internally, the body gets weaker with each crash. A good recovery program is not measured only by the speed of recovery, but also by the absence of adrenal crashes along the way.

If not properly nurtured back to full function, these small crashes become more frequent and intense. Over time, as the body gets weaker, the recovery time also lengthens. This means that if no steps are taken to repair the damage, the body enters Stage 1 of Adrenal Fatigue Syndrome and slowly gets worse, advancing to Stages 2 and 3, and ultimately to adrenal failure. This is why everyone needs to be aware of AFS; understanding stress and the adrenals help us protect the body by living in such a way as to avoid the serious stages of AFS.

Minor crashes might be infrequent during the early stages of AFS (Stages 1 and 2), but can occur every few days in late stages (Stages 3 and 4). *Major* crashes usually occur only once every few years in early AFS, but can occur as frequently as every few weeks in Stage 3. In such cases, the body never has a chance to fully recover, but instead goes through one crash cycle after another. In the absence of corrective steps that nurture the adrenals back to health, the body becomes preoccupied with fighting the crashes, along with trying to recover and function normally.

Recurrent crashes mean that the body's emergency system is frequently reactivated in order to overcome the crash, and the body is in a constant state of alertness. This eventually drains the body of energy, finally leading to a state of chronic fatigue and physical exhaustion. In severe cases (Adrenal Exhaustion, Stage

3C or 3D or beyond), sufferers may be bedridden in a state of what we've heard described as the living dead. Further, on the outside, these individuals often appear normal, but internally they can barely function.

Adrenal Crash and Recovery Cycle Anatomy

The complete crash and recovery cycle is broken down into two phases:

- *Crash Phase*, where the body decompensates with worsening debilitation.
- *Recovery Phase*, where bodily functions are gradually restored to the pre-crash level of function.

The most prominent symptom during the crash phase is fatigue, which results from dysfunctional and dysregulated hormonal and metabolic pathways. Therefore, gauging the energy level during the crash phase gives us the most accurate indication of the severity of the crash over time. We lack laboratory tests to quantify this objectively, but we can say that the more symptoms experienced and the relative intensity of those symptoms indicates the depth and severity of the crash.

The recovery phase is marked by a gradual return to a pre-crash level of adrenal function and energy, with unpleasant symptoms resolving as recovery proceeds.

Looking at the more advanced stages, Stage 3C specifically, the recovery phase is further broken down into a stabilization period followed by one or more mini-recovery cycles, each consisting of a *preparation* period, a *honeymoon* period, and a *plateau* period. Think of these three sequential periods as moving up a set of stairs, as the diagram below illustrates. Overall, successful recovery plans consist of multiple "S" curves in an upward sustained series without major downward crashes interfering.

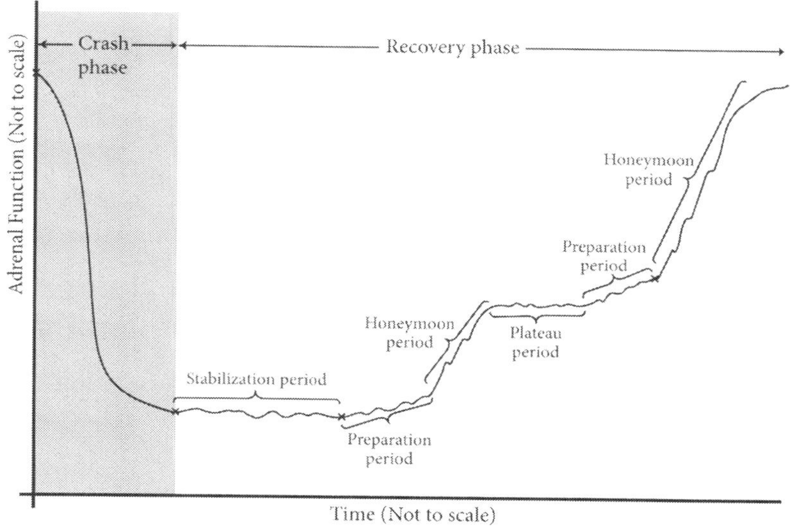

Figure 12. Adrenal Crash and Recovery Curve

The stair step graph above illustrates the following:

Stabilization Period: Immediately after an adrenal crash, and prior to the initial mini-recovery leg up, we usually see a stabilization period during which the body no longer decompensates, but instead, gradually settles into a steady state of lowered function. As we shall see, this stabilization period plays a significant role in the overall recovery phase. We understand that a person is relieved that the worst is over, but we also caution that the unpleasant symptoms can come back at any time.

Preparation Period: Depending on the stage of AFS, this period normally lasts from a few hours to a few weeks. When adrenal function is strong, as in early stages, the duration is short. During this time, sufferers may not feel any significant energy difference, even if they are taking new supplements or increased dosages of current supplements. However, they often feel a sense of improved control, along with a much lessened sense of impending doom. Although the fatigue continues, if individuals pay attention, they experience subtle improvement. In this phase, the body builds its lost reserve and becomes stronger internally. However, it's not uncommon to feel worse from time to time.

Honeymoon Period: Usually following the preparation period, this period can last a few days to weeks—if the preparation period is carried out properly. Here, too, the duration is highly dependent on the stage of AFS, and generally speaking, the earlier the stage the longer this period can last. The weaker the adrenal function, the more short-lived this period tends to be, unless patients are guided by experienced clinicians. During this time the body is better able to handle stress; we see reduced fatigue, heart palpitations and brain fog often dissipate, anxiety attacks diminish, blood pressure begins to stabilize, and functional sleep returns.

We might see mini-crashes and setbacks from time to time that last a few days. Many find these more tolerable than previous mini-crashes, and recovery is faster. Sufferers often report an overall sense of well being, as if a burden has been lifted from their shoulders, and they tend to generally be optimistic again.

Plateau Period: Here, the body has stabilized. The duration of the plateau varies, from a few weeks to a few months or more.

In early stages of Adrenal Fatigue Syndrome, this generally asymptomatic phase can go on for years, but in later stages, we see a more dismal picture. For example, sufferers must slowly adapt to an overall lower energy level. If adrenal function is already at its maximum point, then individuals can be stuck, without upward progress, for a long time.

We also see that many on self-guided programs are unable to rise to the next cycle, because they lack the knowledge needed for ample foresight and planning. Perhaps the most trying time in the recovery cycle, sufferers often grow impatient, usually because they interpret the lack of continued and sustained improvement as failure.

The temptation is to jump from one doctor to another in search of quick results. Especially among those with advanced weakness, most Adrenal Fatigue Syndrome sufferers go through multiple crash and recovery cycles over time. If we carefully analyze and compare triggers and accompanying symptoms of each cycle over time, we are often able to gauge overall adrenal function.

Looking for Causes of Adrenal Crashes

If we look deep enough, we can see that all adrenal crashes are precipitated by some kind of stressor event. Some might appear obvious, such as the death of a loved one or a major life change, such as loss of a job, a relationship, or a home. Or, the event is minor and frequently overlooked, such as taking an extra long walk, a sugar binge, or working a day or two of overtime.

Although small crashes often elude detection, it's extremely important that we investigate the cause of each crash, because history is likely to repeat itself and the same stressor will predictably trigger subsequent crashes. We must understand what triggered the current crash and take steps to prevent recurrence.

Throughout this book, we list various causes of AFS and the kinds of stressors that come into play. Just to emphasize the point that any kind of stress can trigger a crash, we've added another sample list of *everyday* situational stressors that can trigger adrenal crashes. They include: overwork; dehydration; long road trips; vacation; dental procedures; infection; overexposure to sun; lack of sleep; for males, sexual intercourse with ejaculation; drinking soda or coffee; medication withdrawals, especially steroids; thyroid medication sensitivity, especially T3; infection such as the flu or those caused by insect bites; overmedication, such as the use of steroids and anesthesia with epinephrine; and investigative procedures such as an ACTH stimulation test.

Still more stressor triggers include: overuse of stimulating supplements, heavy metal toxicity, excessive exercise, exposure to heat such as sauna or steam room, exposure to toxic fumes, prolonged standing, becoming overly anxious, relationship difficulties, long airplane trips, moving/relocating, overly aggressive detoxification such as enemas or high colonic treatments, certain kinds of massages or acupuncture, excessive improper breathing and use of stimulating breathing exercises, and stimulating entertainment, such as watching an action movie or riding a roller coaster.

Note: The more advanced the Adrenal Fatigue Syndrome, the less intense the stressor needs to be in order to trigger an adrenal crash. In advanced AFS, the body's reserve is already low. It does not take much to trigger a crash.

In day-to-day life, it's fair to say that many of us are sometimes puzzled by our inability to handle certain kinds of events/stress like we used to. Sometimes people chalk the symptoms up to aging, but other times this essential change leads some to resolve to take better care of themselves or learn to handle stress better. This is a good instinct, but it might lead to self-guided programs or medical diagnoses that end up worsening the AFS.

Symptoms of an Adrenal Crash

Remember that not all adrenal crashes and recovery cycles are symptomatic. As we've said, it's likely that those experiencing Stage 1 and early Stage 2 AFS remain unaware of the crash, especially if sufficient adrenal reserves exist to compensate and ensure normal daily function. These stages can easily last for decades, or in situations of acute stress, the crashes may intensify, occur more frequently, and affect ever greater areas of one's life.

For those in Stages 3 and 4 of Adrenal Fatigue Syndrome, symptoms of varying severity are universally present in a crash. In these stages, symptoms of adrenal crash represent a sudden intensification or abrupt onset of many already existing pre-crash AFS symptoms. As you can see, these match the symptoms listed early in this book. Symptoms can include:

- Drastically reduced energy and increased fatigue.
- Drastic increases in brain fog and dizziness.

- Increased frequent hypoglycemic episodes, as sugar regulation becomes dysfunctional, with accompanying lightheadedness.
- Major change in mental and cognitive function, triggering severe depression, anxiety, irritability, and rage.
- Loss of the steroid hormone precursor DHEA, leading to low testosterone or imbalanced estrogen and progesterone levels. These hormonal changes are often seen in women as sudden increases in symptoms of estrogen dominance appear, i.e., water retention, hot flashes, insomnia, bloating, and emotional changes. In men, libido diminishes greatly.
- Poor digestion from the constant decrease of metabolism, with irregular bowel movements, constipation, and irritable bowel.
- Sudden onset of myalgia with joint pain as the body enters a catabolic (breakdown) state.
- Sudden worsening of symptoms of hypothyroidism, linked with the inhibition of thyroid hormone activation and also suppression of the controlled release of hormones from the thyroid. Dry skin and weight gain are common.
- The sensation of being wired-and-tired is common, with the inability to fall asleep.
- Metabolic imbalance and sugar dysregulation, with bouts of awakening in the middle of the night with cold sweats, palpitations, and hunger pangs.

- Arthritis flare-ups from the poorly regulated inflammatory pathways.
- Acne and hair loss from imbalance in hormones and poor immune response.

An adrenal crash doesn't necessarily include all of these symptoms, and some individuals have only a few, but the symptoms can be severe. Again, generally speaking, the more intense the symptoms, the more severe the crash. One can experience any degree of adrenal crash at any stage of Adrenal Fatigue Syndrome. We also can classify crash intensity into five levels.

The Levels of Adrenal Crash Intensity

Clinically, Adrenal Fatigue Syndrome crashes are classified into 5 levels based on subjective evaluation. This means that clinicians assign certain percentages of function, but patients are not expected to think in those same clinical terms. Rather, patients may describe how they feel, which clinicians then fit into the levels discussed below. However, for both clinicians and patients, these levels are subjective and few individuals are able to put percentages to their adrenal function. We consider levels 1 and 2 minor crashes with good recovery potential; levels 3, 4, and 5 are considered major crashes and hence, the recovery phase is less certain.

Level 1: There is a loss of 10-19 percent of immediate pre-crash baseline level of adrenal function in terms of energy, metabolic imbalance such as hypoglycemia, and emotional dysfunction such as irritability. Typically, sufferers say they are more tired than usual, more irritable, and they experience hunger before meals earlier than normal. These individuals can perform normally at their jobs and complete their household chores, but they feel quite tired at the end of the day. A nap or extra rest helps restore their well-being.

Level 2: There is a loss of 20-29 percent of immediate pre-crash baseline level of function mentioned above. Here, too, we typically see a definite reduction in energy, but at this level taking a nap or resting for thirty minutes is helpful. Many individuals report they are less emotionally stable than normal, and they find themselves easily irritated. They often feel relief when mealtime comes around. By this time, the ability to perform on the job or complete chores is compromised, but when individuals force themselves they can meet their obligations. Even with extra rest during the day, these individuals feel tired and they sense that something is not quite the same. The body is under strain.

Level 3: We see a loss of 30-39 percent of immediate pre-crash baseline level of function as discussed above. Typically, at this point, the energy level is low throughout the day. Extra rest and a nap are not as helpful, and the body remains very tired. By this time, we see moderate reductions in the ability to perform outside activities and household chores. At this level, individuals feel like staying home all day—not only for a few hours to rest. Emotionally, it's common to be short tempered and feel anger and rage. At times, the body craves sugar for energy. Insomnia is worse, and in many cases accompanied by cold sweats, heart palpitations, and dizziness in the middle of the night for no apparent reason.

Level 4: We see a loss of 40-49 percent of immediate pre-crash baseline level of function as discussed above. Typically, fatigue is severe throughout the day, and individuals are unable to perform most household chores. The body feels totally drained, and on an emotional level, individuals often feel depressed—

sometimes, they're too emotionally weak and drained to get angry.

At this level, foods or nutritional supplements that once generated energy can make things worse. It's also characteristic to be unable to work or accomplish regular chores. In some cases, those who work are unable to keep their jobs. Irritability is high, and even TV noise can be very bothersome. Once in bed, the temptation is to stay in bed most of the time as the least draining experience.

Level 5: We see a loss of greater than 50 percent of immediate pre-crash baseline level of function as discussed above. At this level, individuals are bedridden most of the time, getting up only to accomplish the basic personal hygiene chores. It is not unusual to require assistance to walk around the house or even to take a shower or change clothes.

Adrenal Recovery Phase

The recovery phase covers the time from the peak of the crash when the energy is lowest until the body returns to its immediate pre-crash level of adrenal function and energy level. The recovery phase is harder to detect; it can be fast or slow, with frequent setbacks. The more advanced the adrenal fatigue, the less chance we see for a 100 percent recovery.

Under ideal or professionally managed conditions, the recovery phase is marked by multiple mini-cycles each consisting of three components: preparation, honeymoon, and plateau. Each mini-cycle can range from a few days to a few weeks. The weaker the adrenals, the more such mini-cycles are needed and the longer each mini-cycle will last in order to return to pre-crash levels of function. If not handled properly, such mini-cycles may also be a setup for follow up rolling crashes.

Even in successful recovery, post-recovery energy is generally still below the level of pre-crash levels, and a second or third dip or setbacks are common during the entire recovery process. For some, we see a prolonged period of stabilization before the first recovery mini-cycle begins, especially among those with Adrenal Fatigue Syndrome Stage 3 or beyond. At the extreme, some do not recover at all but instead progress to the next crash after a period of stabilization.

Over time however, we usually can detect a definite recovery phase following each major crash. The following figure shows the various possible recovery curves.

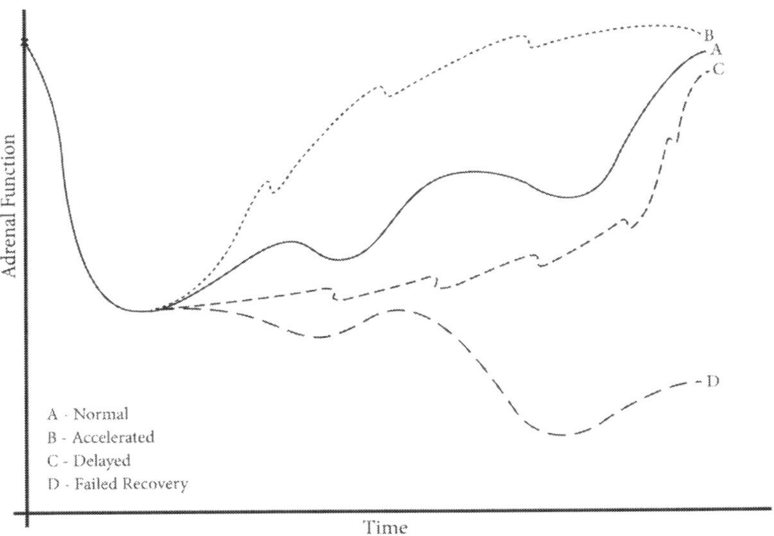

Figure 13. A Comparison of Adrenal Function Recovery Curves

Curve A represents a normal recovery with many mini-recovery cycles along with inevitable setbacks, but a gradual up trend in adrenal function.

Curve B represents an accelerated recovery usually occurring in those in Stages 1 and 2, or those with very strong constitution. We also associate this curve with those who are able to go from the crash phase to honeymoon period directly, usually under professional guidance. This is the most desirable curve.

Curve C represents a prolonged stabilization period and delayed recovery common in Stage 3.

Curve D represents a failed recovery after a moderate stabilization period. We see progression to a subsequent adrenal crash, which is common among those with weak constitutions. This is the least desirable.

All four types of recovery curve are possible in any stage of AFS, although the delayed (curve C) and failed (curve D) are more prominent in the more advanced stages of adrenal weakness as well as those with weak constitution. Unless stressors are removed and the adrenal glands are given the correct tools and nurtured back to health naturally, most recoveries are eventually followed by subsequent worsening crashes as part of the natural progression of this condition.

Common Signs of Adrenal Recovery

Signs of adrenal recovery include:

- Symptoms of the crash appear to be stabilizing, or at least not worsening.
- A sense of calm returns, along with a better ability to deal with stress.
- Reduced anxiety.
- Reduced sense of hypoglycemia.
- More energy for ordinary activities impossible during a crash (i.e., washing dishes or gardening).

- Less salt craving.
- Temporary *worsening* of estrogen dominance symptoms such as PMS and heavy menstrual bleeding.
- Temporary rejection of nutritional supplements that had been beneficial previously.
- Sudden positive and exaggerated response to nutrients, but followed by negative response.
- Return of dreaming during sleep.
- Return of menstrual period where there was amenorrhea (no menstrual cycle) before.

Individuals can have any number of minor or major crashes during any stage of Adrenal Fatigue Syndrome, but those in Stage 3 are the most confusing and difficult to understand. The question is how to manage these distressing situations and begin the process of recovery, which we address in Part II of the main book *Adrenal Fatigue Syndrome: Reclaim Your Energy and Vitality with Clinically Proven Natural Programs.*

Key Points to Remember

- Crashes are very common and inevitable for those in Stage 3 or higher Adrenal Fatigue Syndrome.
- Extreme fatigue is the hallmark of a crash. This is the body's way of forcing a return to a simpler state of survival, i.e. incapacitation. The body's ability to cope with complexity has been overwhelmed.

- A crash is usually followed by a recovery. The recovery phase is further divided into the stabilization, preparation, and honeymoon periods.
- Additional symptoms of an adrenal crash can include worsening hypoglycemia, depression, anxiety, fragile blood pressure, heart palpitations, poor digestion, feeling wired-and-tired, and pain of unknown origin.
- Crash intensity can be categorized into levels 1 to 5, with level 5 being the most serious where over 50 percent of immediate pre-crash function in terms of energy is lost.
- Recovery patterns can be normal, accelerated, delayed, or failed. The most ideal is the accelerated path which normally occurs under professional supervision.
- Common signs of recovery include reduced anxiety, increased energy, reduced salt craving, better sleep, and a sense of calm returning.

Chapter 5

Managing Adrenal Crashes and Recovery

Because adrenal crashes are invariably part of the recovery process, it is imperative that we have a comprehensive plan in place specifically to handle crashes and subsequent recovery. This chapter focuses on special tools and other considerations we use to minimize crashes and maximize the recovery potential.

The key to successfully managing an adrenal crash entails efforts to reduce the velocity and intensity of the crash, and to administer the right nutrients at the right time in order to propel the system into stabilization and follow up recovery as soon as possible. *Minor* adrenal crashes in Stages 1 and 2 usually go unnoticed, but all crashes are noticeable in Stages 3 and 4 of Adrenal Fatigue Syndrome. Crashes involving a loss of 30 percent (level 3 or higher) or more of pre-crash energy are considered major events and can be devastating at any stage.

As AFS advances, the body has less reserve, and the crashes are faster in onset and intensity, if all else is equal. The same stressor that takes a few days to trigger a crash in those with Stages 1 and 2 may take only a few hours or minutes to cause the same damage in those with Stage 3 and 4 Adrenal Exhaustion. In the later stages, symptoms become greatly magnified as well. Effective crash management requires individualized attention. What might be right for one person might actually make another person worse.

We must address the following key areas during crash management:

- ***Physical Activity:*** Usually, sufferers immediately reduce unnecessary physical activity and increase rest. It is important to adjust activity levels to match the energy state of the body during the crash. Those in early AFS may actually find exercising invigorating because exercise increases adrenaline release and improves blood circulation. Those with more advanced AFS, on the other hand, may find any attempt to exercise draining, to say the least. Some can still walk and perform household chores, while others need to take time off and rest. For those with the most severe AFS, bed rest is the only option. In general, all exercise should be reduced and followed by adequate post-exercise rest. Over exercise can drain the body, leading to delayed recovery. While we caution against over-exercise, complete bed rest is not necessarily the best path either.

  It's helpful to begin a personalized program of Adrenal Restorative Exercises and Adrenal Breathing Exercises (described earlier in Chapter 27, *Adrenal Fatigue Syndrome and Healing Exercise* of the main book *Adrenal Fatigue Syndrome: Reclaim Your Energy and Vitality with Clinically Proven Natural Programs*). Because the body is sensitive to even the slightest stress, to avoid triggering further crashes, sufferers must be careful to adjust the intensity and frequency of these exercises to match the body's state. Improper breathing techniques, such as holding the breath for prolonged periods or breathing too deeply, can also increase sympathetic tone and worsen existing crashes.

- ***Dietary Adjustments:*** Hypoglycemia and metabolic imbalances are common during an adrenal crash (Stages 3+), so sufferers must focus their diet on stabilizing blood sugar by balancing the amount of macronutrients (carbohydrate, protein, and fat). In addition, gastric assimilation is often compromised during a crash, so it is important to consider the best way to deliver the macronutrients for maximize absorption. For example, raw milk (where permitted) may be superior to regular milk, and raw egg is better than cooked egg in such cases.

  Those who have had severe crashes might not be able to tolerate regular food; these individuals often need to be on a diet of soups (Chapter 24, *Soups and Juicing for Health* of the main book *Adrenal Fatigue Syndrome: Reclaim Your Energy and Vitality with Clinically Proven Natural Programs*) for foundational nutritional support. Those who are in late, severe AFS stages might actually need to be hospitalized and given total parenteral nutrition, where nutrients are delivered directly into the bloodstream.

- ***Electrolyte Adjustments:*** Salt craving is a common symptom of AFS and can be caused by the sodium imbalance that results from hormonal dysfunction. This imbalance is usually worse during a crash, so to avoid exacerbating the situation, rebalancing must be carefully controlled. Too much sodium relative to water may lead to hypertension and too little water may lead to dehydration, thereby compounding the crash. Too much water relative to sodium may lead to inadequate sodium in the blood. All are undesirable and may be problematic. Unfortunately, laboratory values may be normal during the crash and may or may not be abnormal until the crash is well advanced or much later. Those on diuretics or other medications and who also have a history of high blood pressure need to be especially careful. Symptoms such as nausea, vomiting, headache, malaise, and foggy thinking are common. Severe cases may need hospital admission.

- ***Nutritional Supplement Adjustments:*** Taking nutrients during an adrenal crash requires great care, because AFS can worsen if patients blindly take the same dosage of supplements *during* a crash as they took *before* the crash. The body is in a very different state during a crash. For example, animals under stress need up to ten times more vitamin C than they normally do.

  Various factors determine the amount of key nutrients needed during a crash, including: biological constitution, clearance state, history of paradoxical reactions, and autonomic nervous system sensitivity. There is no one-size-fits-all recommendation, because none exists. For this reason, we recommend you consult your health practitioner for supplementation recommendation when you are experiencing a crash.

Trial and Error

During a crash, the body first goes through a series of adaptations in order to return to homeostasis. When this fails, various internal emergency systems are automatically activated. The more intense the crash, the more such response becomes evident and exaggerated. As the crash progresses, unpleasant and paradoxical symptoms worsen as fatigue accelerates. At the peak of the crash, one may become bedridden for days or even weeks.

Except for those who have very weak constitutions or unresolved stressors, usually the body is eventually able to regain some level of internal control with time. It then enters a stabilization period, followed by a preparation period before the body starts its honeymoon period of recovery.

During the crash, the body is actually hungry for more nutrients to overcome stress, and in its effort to soften the crash, much internal reserve is used and metabolized. Once used, nutrients need to be replenished as quickly as possible, and we may need to consider additional nutrients to support the body during this time. Unfortunately, during AFS, the body is usually also in a low clearance state. In an effort to conserve remaining energy, many organ systems enter a slow down mode. The result is that there is further weakness in gastric absorption and reduced rate of liver detoxification. As excretory capacity is compromised, breakdown byproducts accumulate within the body and can turn toxic. Symptoms such as brain fog, joint pain, muscle ache, and so forth, are more common and intense.

This forms a vicious cycle. If not properly managed, things can get worse quickly. In particular, if extra nutrients are administered during a time of stress and low clearance, a variety of toxic and paradoxical reactions may arise. In other words, instead of getting better, the crash worsens.

Because crashes are inherently complex, expect some trial and error even in the best of hands, because the underlying physiology is still poorly understood. On the other hand, although an adrenal crash is one of the most difficult events to manage in AFS, we often see a silver lining.

Recovery Management

The adrenal crash phase usually takes a few hours to a few days to complete its course. It is one of the most dreaded experiences.

The ensuing recovery phase, however, usually takes much longer—often weeks and sometimes months. Those with weak constitutions are especially vulnerable to an overall delayed recovery phase. This is why it is critically important during any recovery program to avoid crashes at all times. There are no good crashes, as every crash is damaging to the body. We are proactive in our program to prevent crashes rather than reactive and play catch-up afterwards. The absence of crashes is, therefore, a sign of good recovery.

The main focus of adrenal crash management involves reducing crash intensity and duration, analogous to quickly assembling a safety net to soften the harsh landing of a person falling. On the other hand, in recovery management our focus involves providing the body with enough tools for it to heal itself.

Adrenal recovery management is analogous to leading a blind man across a stream, wisely moving slowly and gently. One foot is always ahead trying to feel where and how secure the next rock is before actually putting body weight on it. That is how one avoids falling into the water, or in the case of adrenal recovery, crashing again. There is nothing worse than rolling crashes, where one crash is followed by another one. In such cases, the body hardly gets a chance to recover properly.

For sure, the recovery process is a long distance run, not a sprint. It requires systematic planning, training, testing, and allowing for setbacks. Imagine training for a marathon. At first you may simply walk to the finish line to gauge your energy reserve when you have completed the course. If that is successful, you then slowly work to higher speeds. Most successful marathon training programs stress a gradual approach, with intermittent challenge runs along the way to gauge your body's reserve and energy level. The recovery plan from adrenal crashes is similar.

The body is not a light switch that can be turned on and off at will. AFS often takes years to develop, so it may need ample time to heal itself. Some mistakenly focus on a speedy recovery, usually through the use of stimulatory compounds or medications. That ignores the more important goal and concept of rebuilding the underlying reserve. Pushing the body ahead of its readiness is a recipe for future crashes and recovery failure.

A successful recovery management program incorporates the following factors:

Stabilization immediately after an adrenal crash: After a severe crash has occurred, the body goes into a period of stabilization. It is important to manage the body well at this time. Emergency systems triggered during the crash need to be deactivated by reducing the frequency of alarm signal activation. This is best accomplished by properly adjusting diet, lifestyle, and nutritional supplementation to match the functional level of the adrenal system. Although this varies from person to person, we may need more nutrients at certain times and fewer at others. As the body stabilizes, paradoxical reactions gradually resolve and the low clearance state improves. As a result, follow up crashes are less easily triggered.

Prepare the body for the honeymoon period: After stabilization, we evaluate and examine various dysfunctional systems, starting with the most prominent dysregulation. For example, those who have ovarian-adrenal-thyroid (OAT) axis imbalance may be thyroid dominant, meaning their primary symptoms are more related to thyroid dysfunction than ovarian or adrenal irregularity. Similarly, some may have dominant adrenals, prominent sympathetic symptoms, and adrenaline rushes. These individuals are wired-and-tired, a symptom of ANS imbalance.

As much as possible, the priority is to help the body heal the most damaged system. The total recovery process is only as strong as the weakest link. Identifying the most damaged system and prioritizing treatment is, therefore, important.

At times, fatigue can be so overwhelming that sufferers and doctors tend to focus only on regaining energy instead of fixing the underlying dominant dysfunction. It's tempting to fix the worse symptom, usually fatigue, but short term improvement doesn't help identify the weakest link. In fact, it is often masked. For example, low energy could result from low blood sugar or electrolyte imbalance, but these can have different root causes. Low blood sugar can point to metabolic dysregulation; electrolyte imbalance could point to aldosterone insufficiency. So, boosting energy alone is not going to help the adrenal recover over time.

Most people present multiple symptoms that require careful analysis. If energy is good in the morning, but fatigue sets in late in the afternoon, then modulating the blood sugar level is a priority. This is in contrast to taking steroids or other stimulants to prop up energy levels. Without proper normalization, the body struggles every day to maintain homeostasis, and lacks reserves to rebuild itself. As a result, it is unable to enter the honeymoon phase with vigor, and recovery will invariably be delayed or fail over time. Those who fail to prepare and plan for a sustained recovery are in effect preparing themselves to fail.

Take properly dosed nutrients to match adrenal function for recovery: In addition to identifying the most prominent dysfunction for action, it is important to note that such dominance can change along the recovery path. A good clinician is always on the lookout for this. For example, we may see a prolonged period of stabilization without significant improvement and then suddenly the person improves. The body may also go through sudden turbulent periods for no apparent reasons, reacting erratically and negatively to a once helpful supplement. Astute clinicians need to be on special alert to quickly adjust nutrients to match the body's specific needs each step along the way. Identifying and titrating nutrient dosages is more of an art than a science, and requires extensive clinical experience.

Prevent follow up crashes that can set back the internal homeostasis: One of the hallmarks of successful recovery is the absence of follow up crashes. Those with advanced AFS or weak constitutions simply cannot afford any crashes at all. The worst recovery pattern possible is the fast recovery followed by many rolling crashes. Therefore, the primary goal is to avoid crashes by giving the body extra supports so that its marginal reserve is increased. The speed of recovery takes a back seat in favor of steady recovery. Nutrient doses that are too large increase the energy, but carry a higher risk of adrenal crash. Multiple crashes over time are a sign of poor recovery, so we make every effort to avoid them.

Prepare a set of tools to prevent, abort, or soften future crashes: Not all nutrients are treated the same way by the body. The adrenal recovery nutritional toolbox should have a good mix of all. The strong ones need to be identified, and used sparingly, while gentle nutrients can be used more frequently. Those particularly well suited for emergency situations are identified and set aside. They form an emergency nutritional kit that the sufferer can reach out to in case of crashes. Having such a kit handy has helped many avoid and better manage their crashes.

A Closer Look at the Recovery

During the *stabilization/plateau period* many patients become discouraged and impatient when their energy levels are not immediately restored. This can go on for months. They believe they are merely treading water. This is perhaps one of the most frustrating times. Many give up on their doctor because they do not feel any improvement.

It must be remembered that the adrenals secrete over 50 different hormones; some act quickly, while others take time. Energy is not the only parameter of recovery, and patience is required. Quick fix stimulants and aggressive use of nutrients put patients at risk of crashes. Driving up energy without proper counterbalances will eventually lead to an overall weaker state of adrenal function.

After each mini-recovery cycle up, we like to see a plateau period, similar to the stabilization period, but it happens only after the honeymoon period and not after an adrenal crash. It is prudent to allow the body to rest during the plateau. After rest and consolidation of energy at this level, the body will be ready for the preparation period, that is, a time to get ready for the next honeymoon period of adrenal recovery. If we don't allow the body this plateau phase, we increase the risk of subsequent crashes.

Resetting State

Oftentimes during the recovery phase, the body may go through a period where it tries to reset and kick start itself for reasons we don't completely understand. Perhaps it is nature's last resort to try to help itself when all else fails. During a crash, the body often goes into an emergency mode. This resetting may be part of the delayed survival mechanism that activates automatically. If resetting occurs, the timing varies from person to person. As we've said, during the resetting, the body suddenly behaves differently for no apparent reason.

This is a turbulent time for the body and is discouraging for patients who may not know what to do next. The resetting state usually occurs sometime during the late initial stabilization period, late in the plateau period, or sometime during the preparation periods of subsequent mini-recovery cycles.

Duration of Adrenal Recovery Phase and Recovery Factor (RF)

So, how long does recovery take?

No single answer exists, but we can say that the length of the recovery phase varies because it is dependent on the stage of AFS. The more advanced the AFS, the longer the recovery phase.

Recovery factor (RF) is a quantitative measurement of the length of the recovery phase relative to the duration of the crash phase. RF is a numerical number derived by dividing the recovery time by the crash time.

If the crash duration is one day and the subsequent recovery time to return to the immediate pre-crash baseline is four days, then RF = 4/1 = 4. In other words, it takes the body four times longer to recover relative to the length of the crash. The more severe the crash and the more advanced the AFS, the larger the number. Those in Stage 3C or higher frequently have a recovery factor of 10 or more. In other words, it takes more than 10 days to recover from one day of crash. You can see why we are so vigilant in preventing crashes.

When Good News Turns Bad

Unfortunately, programs using stimulatory compounds (natural or prescription) may appear to bring about improvement for a short time, and sufferers are misled into believing they've found the right path. Invariably, symptoms return and are worse, and a more severe second crash occurs, which continues the downward cascade of symptoms. The body weakens as additional crashes occur. These crashes propel the body into advanced stages of Adrenal Fatigue Syndrome that could have been avoided if a good recovery program had been followed early on.

Those who do not pay attention to the lessons learned from the recovery phase invariably will miss important clinical perils and thus lack a plan to handle future crashes. The result is a body that is subjected to repeated crashes over time.

Understanding the crash and recovery cycle in detail and their characteristics will help the clinician and sufferer better manage the crash as it happens, prepare a soft landing, set a realistic recovery time, and select the proper tools to effect maximum adrenal healing in the shortest time with minimum risk of triggering a subsequent crash. It also helps the sufferer to understand the natural progression of Adrenal Fatigue Syndrome and to have realistic expectations of the road ahead.

Crash Prevention Tips

We can't always prevent adrenal crashes, but you can use these tips to slow down crashes that may be coming your way:

- Increase Adrenal Breathing Exercises to 5 times a day or more.
- Increase Adrenal Restorative Exercises to 3 times a day.
- Cancel all nonessential activities outside the house.

- Delay dealing with stressors.
- Stay away from refined sugar and watch your diet.
- Maintain your body's hydration by drinking water.
- Increase salt intake to as much as you can tolerate.
- Have a snack every two hours and eat more food if you have signs of hypoglycemia.
- No watching TV, computer surfing.
- Minimize negative thoughts and avoid arguments.
- Avoid alcohol or caffeinated beverages.
- Avoid direct sunlight or prolonged indirect sunlight.
- Take nutritional supplements specific for crashes.
- Avoid over-exercise.
- Avoid any form of massage, sauna, colonics, enemas, cleanses, and detoxification programs.
- No sex.

Overall, stay alert and tune in to your body's needs, signs, and symptoms so you can record any changes that happen and report them to your doctor. This is best done systematically with an adrenal journal which we present in Appendix D.

Key Points to Remember

- A key to success in your adrenal recovery program is to prevent crashes while building adrenal reserve gently. Since some crashes are inevitable, especially if external factors are involved, learning how to manage adrenal crashes and recoveries is critical for all because all adrenal crashes worsen the condition.
- Effective crash management requires individualized attention. The key is to avoid physical activity and allow the body to rest. Proper dietary and nutritional supplement adjustments are usually required. Whether to increase or reduce supplements depends on the kind of crash, the individual constitution, and the stage of AFS. Incorrect applications can worsen the crash.
- Recovery management is much more difficult compared to crash management. The more advanced the AFS, the more complicated this is.
- If done properly, recovery management can be an important stepping stone to help the body prepare and enter the next phase of improvement.
- Duration of the recovery phase as measured by the recovery factor is an important clinical indicator of adrenal function.

Chapter 6

Recovery and the Body's Constitution—What You Can Expect

We are each born with a unique inner body type or *biological constitution*, although we can't measure it with a lab test or see it with a CT scan or an MRI. Given today's focus on standardizing treatments, the issue of constitution is rarely discussed in medical literature or considered in recovery plans. The body constitution reflects our genetic makeup. For example, three adults with strep throat will receive prescriptions for antibiotics and told to take them for a certain number of days. They expect to start feeling better after two or three days on the medication. Patient X fully recovers in a week, patient Y recovers in ten days to two weeks, but Patient Z not only needs three weeks to feel well again, but needs more rest than either Patient X or Y. Although many factors can contribute to shorter or longer recovery, the varying constitutions of the three adults likely play an important role.

Individual constitution plays an important role in everything, from back pain to surgery to the common cold. It's an extremely important concept for all those with Adrenal Fatigue Syndrome, because constitution plays a role in *all* stages and features of AFS. Identifying and understanding our patients' constitution helps us formulate, customize, and manage individual recovery plans. This is why we have devoted a chapter to AFS and body constitution.

When we talk about body type, we're usually describing the body's physical shape, especially as it relates to athletic ability or attractiveness. However, in the context of holistic healing, your body type, or biological constitution, refers to the inner makeup and your ability to deal with illness.

Even the most skilled conventionally trained physicians are unable to physically examine their patients and definitively determine their biological constitution. The biological constitution is a subtle concept and whether we are aware of it or not, it plays an important role in everyday life. For our purposes, we're using the terms "constitution" and "body type" interchangeably, but by any name, our constitution influences the way we metabolize nutrients, digest food, think and process information, both work and play, and sleep.

No two individuals experience the condition in exactly the same way—which is one reason it's difficult to study Adrenal Fatigue Syndrome. The wide varying experience of AFS comes back to body type. We can trace the confusion about AFS back to the variation in response to the same stressors, which influences the level of Adrenal Fatigue Syndrome in a way that often defies medical logic. Some people can be under severe stress and perform well, while others crash under what to some seems like only the slightest stress. Certain individuals with AFS progress slowly but steadily from Stage 1 to Stage 3 over time; others quickly deteriorate and never fully recover. In large part, we can attribute these differences to constitution.

What about Genetics?

We're born with a particular genetic makeup, or *genome*, which determines elements of our body from the obvious anatomical components such as blood, muscle, and organs, to the more subtle internal hormonal and metabolic systems. In fact, anti-aging research has found that about 30 percent of our longevity is determined by our genes, while 70 percent is determined by our diet and lifestyle. Under normal circumstances, the individual genome plays an important role in determining, for example, who gets cancer and who does not. We all know of lifelong chain smokers who never develop lung cancer while nonsmokers in perfect health may develop the disease and die quickly.

Weak parts exist in everyone's constitution because none of us are born perfect. Moreover, some have more weak parts, some less. For example, those with relatively weaker immune systems tend to get sick easily and more frequently. Others might have metabolic weakness, and for them, weight management is a lifelong issue. We have no control over the body type we're born with, but we can nurture our weak parts in order to restore and strengthen them as much as possible.

Recent genetic research illuminates this situation. Although our basic genome does not change over time, its expression does. In other words, as you age, your genes do not change, but your *epigenome* (the biochemical mechanism that turns genes on and off) changes dramatically. Today, epigeneticism has emerged as a factor with primary influence on the way environmental factors such as diet, lifestyle, and stress influence the expression of your genes. In other words, the expression of your genes, not the genes themselves, dictates whether you develop certain diseases.

In the case of the adrenal glands, certain factors can amplify constitutional weakness, including: aging, obesity, excessive childhood illness, prolonged stress, and overuse of antibiotics, just to name a few. The same is true for emotional trauma such as death of a loved one, physical trauma such as a car accident, relational difficulties such as divorce, and psychosomatic illnesses.

If you were born with weak adrenal glands, it's likely that this weakness will be expressed when you're under stress, and this might lead to AFS. On the other hand, the absence of significant stress can delay the expression of this weakness for an indefinite period of time.

If you were born with constitutionally strong adrenal glands, you might not develop AFS despite severe stress. Those with weak adrenal functions might experience symptoms when exposed to stress, even as teenagers. Throughout your life, your genome, along with the epigenome, determines your body's weakest link and subsequent expression of illness.

A Different View: East versus West

Western medicine doesn't have a good understanding of the concept of the body constitution, and therefore, tends to treat all bodies alike, with the exception of certain identified genetic markers such as the genes linked with breast cancer. On the other hand, eastern medical philosophy emphasizes the forces of nature that govern the human body and are responsible for regulating all systemic, endocrine, metabolic, and functional changes in the body. These forces of nature are enveloped in the five vital elements:

- Air, the vital force behind all functions.
- Fire, the source of energy and heat and responsible for transformation, such as metabolism, hormones, and saliva production.

- Earth, the element of strength and anabolism (building up), such as collagen, ligaments, and muscles.
- Water, that which binds structures together, such as urine, sweat, and gastric enzymes.
- Space, where all factors exist, such as the oral cavity, and the respiratory and reproductive system.

For the body to feel good and function normally, all five elements must be in perfect balance. In ayurvedic medicine, the ancient philosophy of health and healing developed in India, the prakriti is the name for the individual biological constitution that remains constant throughout life. The prakriti manifests as individual physical attributes and physiological and psychological responses in line with universal laws. In eastern philosophical thinking, universal laws rule the formation, existence, and destruction of all objects on a space and time continuum of consciousness. Within these laws, every individual is a unique entity, and the prakriti, therefore, is one-of-a-kind.

Whether we look at it from the eastern or western medical perspective, AFS is an expression of how the body deals with stress. The degree of damage and subsequent recovery pattern depends largely on the body's biological constitution. Those with strong adrenal constitutions recover faster and have a longer sustained recovery when compared to those who have weak adrenals. This is in part the reason that many individuals never advance beyond Stages 1 and 2 with severe stress. However, those with weak adrenals might never fully recover after crashes, and these individuals might continue a downward path of decompensation over time.

Unfortunately, no routine laboratory test exists to determine the body's constitution. The best assessment comes from a good narrative history that astute clinicians examine and interpret.

Since advanced AFS generally develops over a period of years, the body usually sends out many signals. However, most people pay little attention to these signals and choose to ignore them or write them off as normal in one context or another. When AFS finally triggers crashes and the body fails to recover, we're at a loss to explain what's happened. Most in advanced AFS can look back at their life retrospectively, and see that invariably their symptoms had been evident for a long time if they only paid attention.

Your Constitution

The pattern of recovery from AFS and the kind of nutrients required differ depending on the type of body constitution. This is why it's important to know from the start if you have a strong, normal, or weak body constitution if you think you have AFS.

You can see from the chart below, constitutions can range from very strong to very weak, with 68 percent falling into the normal range, as shown on a bell curve. The rest of the population falls in the remaining smaller distributions: 14 percent weak, 14 percent strong, 2 percent very weak, 2 percent very strong. (These ranges should not be taken as absolute.)

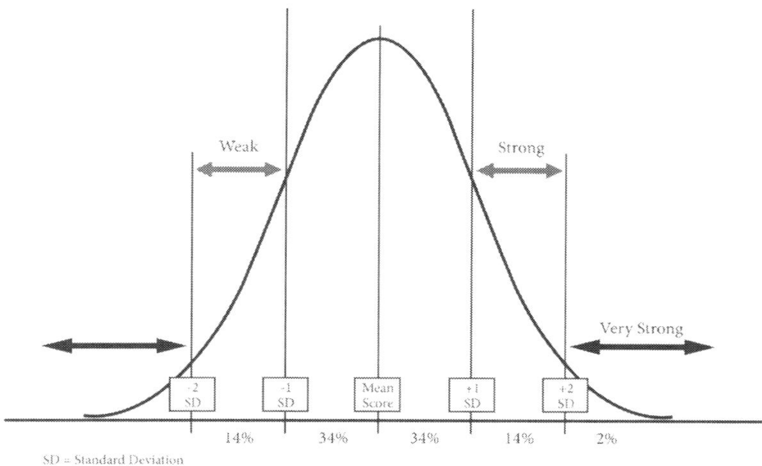

Figure 16. Percentage Distribution of Strong, Normal and Weak Constitutions in the Population

Percentages alone don't tell us much, so we're better off attempting to describe what it means to have a strong or weak constitution.

The constitutionally *very weak* in overall health tend to get minor illnesses frequently and take a long time to get well. They frequently develop seasonal rhinitis or sensitivity to pollen during the spring. They tend to be intolerant to heat during the summer, experience rolling colds and flu during the fall, and are intolerant to cold in the winter. They often have multiple food sensitivities, especially for wheat, dairy, and corn products, and are highly sensitive to both over-the-counter (OTC) or prescription medications. Their gastric system seems to be sensitive to the environment, so they are often more susceptible than normal travelers to travelers' gastroenteritis. Despite these symptoms that affect them most of the time, their routine laboratory tests usually look normal. They frequently visit physicians for one ailment or another, and seem to be always struggling to stay healthy.

On the opposite end of the spectrum, those who are constitutionally *very strong* seem to never get sick, even for one day. They are often described as strong as an ox. They stand up better to viruses and stay healthy when others fall prey. Routine laboratory tests are also within the normal range.

Those who have *strong* overall constitutions are less likely to develop AFS, and if they do, the progression tends to be slower, the adrenal crashes are less intense, and they can recover faster and sustain their recovery.

Those with weak constitutions have a higher propensity to develop AFS, even when they're exposed only to the stresses of normal daily living. In addition, they have higher chances of deteriorating to advanced stages, and their adrenal crashes tend to be more intense, with delayed and protracted recoveries that are difficult to sustain.

Looking back on their lives, most adults can surmise their overall constitutional status. The majority of us fall into the normal range, with our share of common colds, stress, and strain.

Aside from the general biological constitution of the body, each organ has its own constitution too, which explains why many who are constitutionally weak have strong adrenals. The opposite is also true. Therefore, determining the biological constitution of the adrenal glands depends on a host of factors, many of which remain unknown, but these factors certainly include the adrenals' intrinsic constitution and that of other closely related organ systems such as the thyroid and ovarian systems.

Body Constitution and Advanced AFS

Nowhere is the constitution's effect on Adrenal Fatigue Syndrome recovery more prominent than in Stage 3C, the state of disequilibrium (see Chapter 9, *Stage 3C—Disequilibrium* of the main book *Adrenal Fatigue Syndrome: Reclaim Your Energy and Vitality with Clinically Proven Natural Programs*). You will recall that we also refer to Stage 3 and its phases as Adrenal Exhaustion. At this stage we often see concurrent ovarian, adrenal, and thyroid dysfunction (OAT axis imbalance, see Chapter 8, *Stage 3B—Hormonal Axis Imbalances* of the main book *Adrenal Fatigue Syndrome: Reclaim Your Energy and Vitality with Clinically Proven Natural Programs*), along with dysregulation of hormones such as cortisol, adrenaline, norepinephrine, thyroid, insulin, and estrogen. Symptoms include hypoglycemia, moderate to severe fatigue, low blood pressure, anxiety, insomnia, adrenaline rush, heart palpitations, low libido, POTS (postural orthostatic tachycardia syndrome), PMS (premenstrual syndrome), menstrual irregularities, and hypothyroidism.

During this time, the emergency backup system is activated to maintain homeostasis. The autonomic nervous system is on full alert, and the body can be flooded in a sea of adrenaline. For many, this is a wakeup call that their adrenal glands are in deep trouble, with rapidly declining adrenal function.

Being aware of the body's constitution allows for an optimized recovery program for Stage 3C, and is also important because the weaker the constitution, the faster the decline and the slower the recovery.

Failing to factor the weaker constitution into a recovery plan is a common mistake that might delay or worsen the recovery outcome.

The following graph illustrates how the body's constitution affects the recovery phase of Stage 3C Adrenal Fatigue Syndrome recovery:

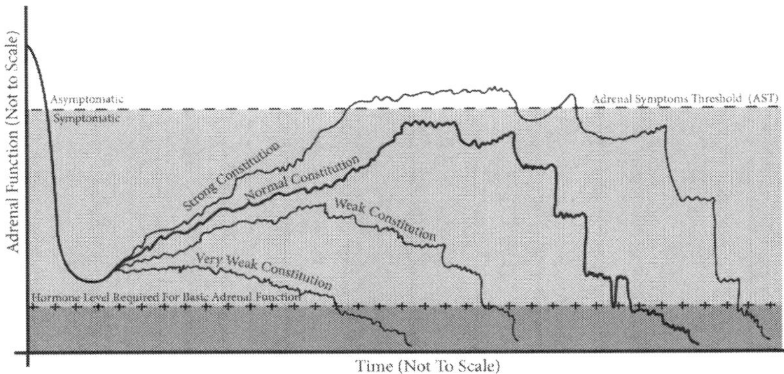

Figure 17. Adrenal Exhaustion Recovery Pattern Based on Body Constitution

It is evident from the above graph that the degree and speed of recovery varies greatly depending on one's constitution. Below, we look in detail at each recovery pattern in relation to the constitution. Refer to the graph above to follow the line.

Very Weak Constitution

Only a small percentage of the general population has a very weak body constitution, but these individuals are the most desperate when afflicted with AFS and no noticeable recovery occurs after an adrenal crash. The body may go through a period of stabilization, but even this is marred with multiple minor crashes along with intermittent major ones where energy drops 30 percent or more compared to the immediate pre-crash level.

Severe symptoms such as hypoglycemia, low blood pressure, and insomnia continue to persist and get worse over time, and normal daily activities are severely disrupted. It is not unusual for these individuals to spend much of their time in bed or on the couch. Many become completely bedridden. Not only has recovery failed, but energy levels continue on a sloping downhill path. Ultimately, some form of crash will occur that pushes the key adrenal hormones and functions below that which is necessary for basic normal adrenal function. The timeframe varies, but we're usually looking at a matter of months, that is, if we fail to make it a priority to quickly nurture the adrenals back to health. Once this crash has occurred, the body declares a state of emergency that keeps only the most basic functions going, but compromises others, such as gastrointestinal and reproductive functions.

Weak Constitution

Those with weak constitutions are likely to experience a noticeable but mild recovery after a major crash when they have progressed into Stage 3C.

We might see a sustained period of gradual improvement, but progress is generally slow. Minor crashes and setbacks are expected along the way. Eventually, the sufferer reaches a plateau in which the person doesn't improve, and more rest doesn't increase the body's energy level. On good days, normal activities can be carried out. However, bad days are quite frequent and extensive rest is needed. In Stage 3C, we can say that the body is marginally functional at best. When a new stressor hits, inevitable crashes follow which lower adrenal functions, much like a series of small downhill steps. A period of stabilization follows each crash; these periods might be accompanied by a gradual reduction in energy levels, or, a better situation, the same energy level is maintained.

Follow-up crashes tend to be increasingly intense and severe, with longer recovery times. If there is no intervention, the body likely will experience a major crash and enter into Stage 3D AFS.

After a brief pause and declining stabilization period, adrenal failure may ensue. As compared to those with very weak constitutions, those in this category are more fortunate because the natural progression of the condition is somewhat slower, thereby allowing patients to experience intermittent periods where they function more normally. Unfortunately, if nothing is done to help the recovery process, a high risk exists for the ultimate outcome, adrenal failure.

Normal Constitution

Most of us find ourselves in this category, one in which Adrenal Fatigue Syndrome comes on slowly and gradually over years or decades. Those in this category are likely unaware they have developed AFS until they enter Stage 3. If a crash does occur, these individuals often are able to mount a reasonable and moderate level of recovery over time. Unfortunately, this cannot be sustained.

After a major crash into Stage 3C, the recovery pattern is characterized by significant energy improvement over time. The body might welcome rest, but it is not necessarily required, because the person's biological constitution is strong enough to sustain some setbacks. Minor crashes surface periodically, but are still manageable. The setbacks tend to be rhythmic in nature. Taking afternoon naps and going to sleep early helps tremendously.

Although a full recovery back to the asymptomatic level above the Adrenal Symptoms Threshold (AST) is usually not possible, recovery may be close to that level. Individuals remain symptomatic below the AST, but are far better than they were at the peak of the crash. Some discomfort is inevitable, but proper rest and lifestyle adjustments can bring about improvement.

Those with normal constitutions need to rest frequently in order to cope with fatigue. The problem is that these individuals are accustomed to full and active lifestyles, and they tend not to change their ways. In fact, most in this category are usually in denial for a long time, even when the body shows signs of being in trouble. Those who have been constitutionally weak all their lives are used to slowing down and taking frequent naps, but those in the normal constitutional range live as fully productive individuals and they generally consider resting only at the end of the day.

The vast majority of us who have normal constitutions struggle to balance work and rest, and even when we seek professional help, we don't necessarily comply with the advice we're given. However, if we don't allow sufficient time to nurture the body back to health, we are creating a setup for subsequent crashes, and with each crash the body tries to mount a recovery effort, which brings relief at first. However, over time, continued crashes weaken the adrenals and influence the recovery curve, which tends to be stable at best.

Ultimately, many crashes followed by flat stabilizations resemble downward stair steps, a process that can last for months and even years. Eventually, the body's reserve is so low that it crashes and likely will enter into Stage 3D Adrenal Fatigue Syndrome. After a final stabilization period, the risk of adrenal failure becomes high.

Strong and Very Strong Constitutions

Those with a strong adrenal constitution usually are able to mount a steady and significant recovery from Stage 3C. The recovery curve is smoother than those with a normal constitution because the body is better able to cope with setbacks. Eventually, the body returns to the level of function above the AST and these individuals become asymptomatic. These fortunate people experience a sustained symptom-free period, but this changes over time.

Some individuals with a strong body constitution recover without intervention and do not experience interruptions in their normal daily functioning. Moreover, they might sustain this asymptomatic period for years. Externally, they appear cured and totally normal, but internally, the body is struggling to stay asymptomatic as it stays marginally above the AST. These individuals recover relatively quickly from occasional minor crashes, characterized by unpleasant but tolerable symptoms.

Stretching into decades, these individuals are usually able to continue their fulltime jobs, and when they are tired, they might try taking various natural compounds designed to boost energy. Because the symptoms are marginal, they don't see a need to visit their physician for help. Eventually, however, the years and decades add up if the chronic stressors are not removed. Then, one of the inevitable major stressful life events comes along, such as the death of a loved one or a major career or financial setback. Because we have a tendency to be ill prepared for this kind of event, it normally comes as a surprise. Sufferers often deny that AFS exists and they continue to push themselves past symptoms.

The Context of Recovery

Our society's Type A climate rewards aggressive personality styles. Generally, Type As also ignore symptoms. We have relied on the idea of quick fixes, such as antibiotics, to name one category of drugs. Until recently, we ignored the pros and cons of their use, their overall effectiveness, and the consequence of microbial resistance that ultimately renders them ineffective. Pharmaceutical companies are involved in a continuous scramble to find new antibiotics.

In the process of finding quick cures, we have lost the concept of convalescence. By that we mean giving the body time to heal from infections and illnesses, like colds and flu.

Out of fear of losing their jobs, employees may be afraid to stay home when they are ill, and even if they do take a couple of days off, they often return too soon, thereby undermining the idea that the body needs rest to fully recover—what we used to call convalescence. Some parents go to work when they're ill in order to save their own sick days to stay home with their children.

Over the long term, this isn't beneficial for individuals or the society, but it's the situation that seems entrenched and is unlikely to change in the near future. The result is the strain on the adrenals is overlooked when we push past the symptoms of illness that tell us the body needs rest.

Since Adrenal Fatigue Syndrome is not a well known condition, the situation tends to become even more complicated. Sufferers lose valuable time that should be used to nurture the body to rebuild the adrenal reserve that is slowly but surely dwindling. Eventually, crashes become more frequent and intense, and recovery becomes less successful and these individuals no longer stay asymptomatic. Unless the downward trend changes, the body may eventually crash into Adrenal Fatigue Syndrome Stage 3D and ultimately risk entering adrenal failure.

The following graph summarizes the various patterns based on constitutional types. As you can see, it shows seven recovery

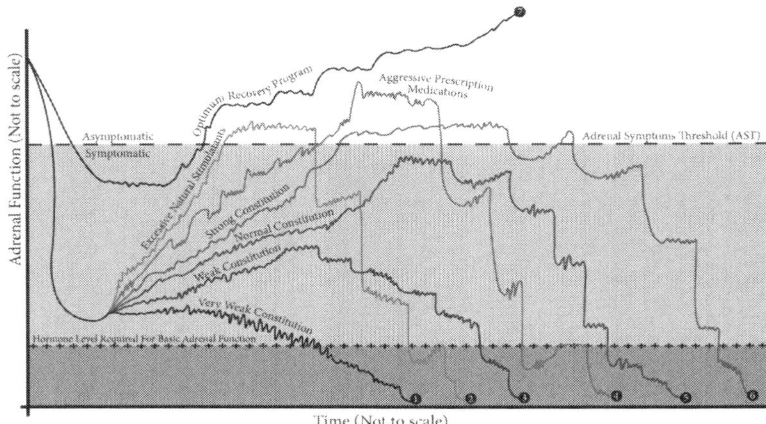

Figure 18. Adrenal Exhaustion Recovery Patterns

Pattern 5 is the most common. Here we see the slow deterioration over time for those who have a normal constitution and suffer Adrenal Fatigue Syndrome.

In Pattern 6, we see that the time can be lengthened if the intrinsic body constitution is strong. It is clear that the stronger you are constitutionally, the slower your overall decline.

In Pattern 3, we see that those with a weak constitution do poorly. Their recovery is often suboptimal, and their decline over time tends to be accelerated when compared to the natural progression.

In Pattern 1, we see clearly that those with a very weak constitution do the worst. Their recovery is characterized by rolling crashes that they never seem to recover from.

In *Pattern 2*, we also see what happens when those who

self-navigate use natural stimulatory compounds excessively or inappropriately. This practice compromises the normal recovery process for most. In *Pattern 4*, we see that aggressive use of prescription medications can worsen the outcome, especially in the presence of a weak constitution. Both Patterns 2 and 4 could leave the sufferer worse off than if nothing is done and nature is allowed to take its course, which we see in Pattern 5. In other words, the person becomes worse, and if this occurs in an individual who has a weak or very weak constitution, then we can expect disastrous results.

In *Pattern 7*, we see what happens with a correctly formulated and personalized recovery program. Any good recovery program attempts to reduce crash intensity, bring about a sustained, robust recovery that is asymptomatic, and reduce the risk of subsequent crashes. So, regardless of constitutional type, we want to mimic the Pattern 7 recovery curve as much as possible.

Barrier to Recovery: Excessive Use of Natural Stimulatory Compounds (*Pattern 2*)

Using natural compounds such as certain herbs and glandulars can be of great help in mild Adrenal Fatigue Syndrome (Stages 1 and 2). However, results can be dangerous for those in Stage 3, Adrenal Exhaustion, if they pursue this strategy without professional guidance. Unfortunately, some in this stage embark on aggressive self-guided programs, exemplified by Pattern 2 in the above graph. Unfortunately, the results can be perilous for the individual in such a program.

After the initial adrenal crash into Stage 3C Adrenal Fatigue Syndrome, recovery results may be promising at first. Recovery is fast and furious as the body's energy level is propped up and sustained with natural compounds. The adrenals are put into overdrive to increase their hormone output and energy returns. Sometimes, the energy level may even return to that above the AST and the sufferer becomes asymptomatic. While the overall energy level may not be the same as pre-crash, unpleasant symptoms are at least not prevalent. The sufferer is misled into thinking that his problem is resolved.

The adrenal glands have a blunted response over time to such a continued stimulation strategy. More natural compounds are needed to have the same sustained energy level. In time, the overall energy level plateaus and fails to increase even with higher dosages. Soon the maximum stimulatory level is reached, at which time the body starts to decompensate. Eventually, the adrenals start to fail, usually precipitated by a stressor triggering the first major crash after a plateau is reached.

After the first major follow up crash, those doing self-guided programs begin to use even more stimulants, believing they need more to avoid another crash. There again may be a period of recovery, but the duration is shorter, and the level of recovery is mild at best, and more crashes follow. With each subsequent crash, the crash intensity is increased. The body's ability to mount a recovery is blunted, and in fact, may slowly decompensate and roll into subsequent crashes, with one crash followed by another. This progression can happen quickly, not far behind those with the very weak constitution mentioned earlier.

Needless to say, this is an undesirable recovery pattern even for those with a normal or strong constitution. Over time, this is a recipe for failure. What the adrenals need are gentle nutrients to nurture themselves back to health, not to be continually put on overdrive without rest, which is what some of these natural compounds may do in those suffering with advanced Adrenal Fatigue Syndrome. It comes as no surprise that this undesirable recovery pattern can only get worse if the constitutional state is weak or very weak.

Barrier to Recovery: Aggressive Use of Prescription Medications (*Pattern 4*)

Physicians commonly prescribe thyroid and/or steroid medications to treat fatigue and low metabolic rates. While these potent drugs have their roles to play, their aggressive use over time can pose a significant risk and, in some, worsen Adrenal Exhaustion. In these situations, recovery tends to progress steadily at first. With each increase in medication potency, dosage, or delivery system, a corresponding increase in energy level appears to immediately follow. This is exemplified in Pattern 4 within Figure 18 on page 102.

Patients and doctors usually are encouraged as fatigue improves and laboratory test results appear to be improving too. As long as the medicine is taken regularly, patients seem to be increasingly asymptomatic, often reaching a peak effect when patients feel as if their bodies are almost back to normal. This situation can continue for a few years. The only problem is that strong medication is needed to keep this energy level sustained. Over time, doctors may add steroid medications in ever increasing doses. However, eventually the adrenals simply cannot be stimulated any further and refuse to cooperate. Eventually a stressor will come, and a major crash follows.

In this situation, physicians unaware of AFS, miss the essential characteristics of the crash, and many doctors tend to increase the dosages of medications, but the response is blunted. At that point, the intensity of the crash increases and recovery efforts are marred, and more crashes follow. Doctors at this time may have exhausted their major arsenal of drugs, and some medications may have even backfired as the patient's symptoms worsened. Patients may be abandoned and may seek help elsewhere, or as often happens, they either go back to self-navigating or they start down that path. Either way, that path frequently ends disastrously at Adrenal Fatigue Syndrome Stage 3D. After a brief and heroic but ultimately unsuccessful attempt to reverse the situation, adrenal failure risk remains high.

Those who fail to improve with prescription medication need to be alert and seek further professional advice.

As expected, those with strong constitutions tend to fair the best even under conditions of treatment error, but those with weak constitutions fair worse. Individuals with very weak constitutions, as described above, often can't tolerate prescription medications. They tend to decompensate the fastest and have the highest risk of adrenal failure.

Recovery Hopes and Complexities

By now, you should have a big picture perspective of Adrenal Fatigue Syndrome. We hope you can see that Mother Nature is always right, and the body does behave logically after all. With this clarity and our alignment with nature, recovery becomes an easier task. We no longer fight our body, but instead give it the tools to heal itself. From our experience, this is the way Mother Nature likes it, and we are wise to follow her lead. In the coming chapters, we examine how natural compounds are used in this quest.

Key Points to Remember

- We are each born with a unique inner type of biological constitution. This determines how strong we are in the presence of external insults. This constitution cannot be detected by laboratory tests, but is generally evident if one reviews the medical history carefully.
- Individual constitution plays an important role in AFS recovery, because those with stronger constitutions usually recover faster than those who are weaker.
- Excessive use of natural stimulatory compounds and aggressive use of prescription medications can be barriers to the recovery process, because they can worsen Adrenal Fatigue Syndrome if not done properly.
- Understanding your symptoms in the context of your constitution allows you to have an honest assessment of your recovery capacity.

Chapter 7

A Total Body Approach to Adrenal Fatigue Syndrome

Medical knowledge of Adrenal Fatigue Syndrome is still in its infancy, and most individuals with the problem are unaware that their symptoms are attributable to AFS. Symptoms of AFS vary so much, and no standardized recovery protocol exists, both of which complicate our understanding of the condition. For these reasons, we see great confusion about how to help those in need.

As practitioners, we have gained clinical expertise over time by handling many severe cases of AFS. Fortunately, the recovery toolbox contains many tools, including a variety of medications, hormones, glandulars, herbs, vitamins, dietary guidelines, and combinations thereof, plus lifestyle tools, including exercise regimens, achieving optimal sleep, and so forth. Despite this comprehensive arsenal of recovery tools, complete Adrenal Fatigue Syndrome recovery remains elusive and for many unattainable. This has led to a common misconception that once seriously afflicted with AFS, it is virtually impossible to overcome.

As we've said, AFS as a condition is under investigated. In addition, mild AFS often goes undetected because symptoms arise intermittently and lack a consistent pattern. However, if properly guided, sufferers usually recover within a relatively short time. Even some self navigation efforts can be effective, as long as the body still has reserves and is able to tolerate trial and error recovery attempts without crashes or setbacks. On the other hand, advanced Adrenal Fatigue Syndrome may leave many individuals housebound and even bedridden. In these cases, proper recovery requires extensive clinical experience and patience, taking into account the body's depleted reserves and high levels of sensitivity.

We see many women and men with severe AFS because they come to us for nutritional coaching as a last resort, usually because conventional medicine and traditional naturopathic ways have failed. Some had never heard of AFS when they found their way to us, and these advanced cases served to educate us about the best ways to help those afflicted.

Our philosophical approach to AFS involves four foundational principles, which we incorporate into a systematic personalized program. What works for patient X might be wrong for patient Y. In any case, our program integrates conventional and holistic strategies into a comprehensive natural healing strategy we call the *Total Body Approach*.

The Four Principles of the Total Body Approach

FIRST: We believe the body is a closed ecosystem capable of self-maintenance and self-healing under normal circumstances.

When stressors overwhelm our internal repair mechanism, breakdown occurs. These stressors can be acute or chronic, physical or emotional, but they are excessive and cause the body to decompensate. Symptoms surface as warning signs of internal disturbances in normal functions; the weakest organ system often is the first one to give way. For example, those with constitutionally weak adrenals relative to other, stronger organ systems may manifest Adrenal Fatigue Syndrome. Likewise, those with weaker cardiovascular systems may develop heart problems, and those with a weak gastric system might develop gastric ulcers. This explains why some people can have severe stress but no Adrenal Fatigue Syndrome.

That said, once severe stress triggers the decompensation cascade of one system, many other systems become sequentially affected. This occurs because the body is not a collection of separate organ systems. Rather, they are all linked internally through many hormonal axes. A disturbance in one system starts a domino effect that results in a potentially overwhelming convolution of symptoms concurrently involving many body systems. This is why in those with advanced AFS we often see symptoms like insomnia, depression, arrhythmia, hypoglycemia, irregular menses, and hypothyroidism. In general, the weaker the adrenals, the more prevalent the symptoms. Although some symptoms such as salt cravings and hypoglycemia are principally caused by adrenal dysfunction, many other symptoms such as arrhythmia and depression are due to the breakdown of other organ systems that had been normal.

SECOND: Mild Adrenal Fatigue Syndrome generally manifests as lack of physical energy, but advanced AFS usually manifests as a mind-body condition rather than solely a physical dysfunction.

The brain ultimately controls the adrenal function by way of the hypothalamic-pituitary-adrenal (HPA) axis and a variety of chemical messengers. Our emotional states have a big impact on adrenal function. Common organ systems that are targets of mind-body disturbances include components of the nervous system, plus the endocrine and metabolic systems. Because knowledge of these systems helps us understand the connection between symptoms, we discuss them throughout this book. Our scientific perspective calls for evaluating each person's unique history, constitution, environment, emotions and mental state, and nutritional status, plus the often convoluted and pressing symptoms, as a whole unit rather than as unrelated parts. This provides a complete picture of the overall clinical state. Ultimately, the best nutritional solution provides both physical and mental health support.

THIRD: We view symptoms as our friends, not our enemies.

Symptoms are the only way the body can tell us what it wants us to do. In our view, we need to allow symptoms to manifest in a controlled environment with minimal discomfort. For example, many symptoms of AFS, such as salt cravings, hypotension (low blood pressure), palpitations, adrenaline rush, anxiety, and hypoglycemia tend to improve when the adrenals are returned to health.

As long as the body is not in acute crisis, we should gently support it while giving it a chance to heal itself. At the same time, we gain insight into the body by observing symptoms during recovery.

This does not mean that we allow unpleasant symptoms to continue unchecked, but we consciously avoid the trap of focusing only on alleviating symptoms. We keep our eyes on the big picture and use symptoms to guide us and support the adrenal's internal healing process nutritionally. The goal is to strengthen the adrenals and prevent future problems.

We seldom see long term success with overzealous recovery strategies based on addressing symptoms rather than nurturing the body back to health, and for good reason. Since symptoms are signs of underlying dysfunction, suppressing symptoms in one system might trigger dysfunction in another system, but often subclinically.

Symptoms soon become even more convoluted and overwhelming when one dysfunction is superimposed on another. We often see this as a side effect of the recovery effort, particularly when conventionally trained physicians prescribe medications that produce side effects. This is a major problem, and the more medications prescribed, the greater the risk of side effects.

FOURTH: We let our body educate us at every opportunity so we know what it wants.

We closely monitor the side effects and potential harm coming from well intentioned nutritional strategy to which each body reacts differently. Our body teaches us every day of its likes and dislikes, if only we listen closely. The more we learn, the better we are able to effectively self navigate. Most of us are not in tune enough with our body. We therefore focus on educating sufferers about their individual body types and what factors they must adjust to in order to return to health and maintain health. We teach them how to listen to and interpret the body's signs, and we educate them to live harmoniously with their body as they take control of their health. We also make sure they understand the pros and cons of each tool in the toolbox, the reasons to use the tool, and what possible negative side effects to look for. As you can see, we devote our energy to *educating* rather than *medicating*.

The Seven Steps of the Total Body Approach

Using the four guiding principles, here are seven specific steps we use to formulate and personalize our Total Body Approach.

Step 1: Know the Body

We take the time to develop an in-depth understanding of the body and its constitutional state, and no shortcut exists to establish this foundation. We confirm this qualitatively through our customized nutritional plan that gently tests and challenges the body while simultaneously nurturing it. By noting each body's unique response, we are able to further personalize a plan specific to that body's needs. In this way, we facilitate recovery.

Although a painstaking and time-consuming process, we've found it the fastest way to facilitate overall recovery. The insights we gain help us avoid the risk of future crashes, which are major setbacks for any recovery program. Overall, we reduce total recovery time, and the healing process is more pleasant.

Step 2: Establish the Dominant Dysfunction

To fully anticipate the body's reaction to any single component of our Total Body Approach, whether it is a nutrient or the diet, *we identify each person's major intrinsic root weakness.* The body as one unit is only as strong as the weakest organ system. The weakest system is also usually the first system to be symptomatic, and thus, the dominant dysfunction. Each person usually has one weakness that is uniquely more susceptible to insult, comparatively speaking. For some, the thyroid may be the weakness, and hypothyroidism may be the first sign of internal weakness. For others, it may be gastric discomfort. For some, it may be the cardiac system, with hypertension as the first sign. The organ system with the most dominant dysfunction is also the weakest link to the entire recovery effort. Therefore, it is important to identify and help the body—naturally and nutritionally—deal with the dominant root cause. Knowing the prominent dysfunction helps us to personalize a recovery program with maximum chances of success.

For example, the natural compound *GABA* (a neurotransmitter that regulates anxiety and sleep) is generally a good sleep aid for those who are adrenal dominant, but it's not as effective for the thyroid dominant. Thyroid dominant individuals generally do well taking 5-HTP (an amino acid that's a precursor to serotonin, a neurotransmitter) to help them sleep. Each nutrient has its own best-use pathway, and for maximum effectiveness, it must be matched to the correct condition.

As for diet, thyroid dominant types benefit most from a vegetarian diet with increased fiber load to enhance gastric assimilation. On the other hand, the ovarian dominant type usually benefits from a diet high in protein relative to carbohydrates. The adrenal dominant type usually does best on a balanced diet with a slight bias toward more protein and fat, along with higher meal frequency to overcome hypoglycemia. Those with a mixed type require a combination of the above.

In terms of exercise, thyroid dominant types usually do best with rhythmic exercise like running/walking, bicycling, or swimming. Ovarian dominant types do best with more gentle and mentally focused exercise such as yoga. The adrenal dominant type is trickier because we can divide them into two main categories: those with high adrenal function and those with low adrenal function. Strenuous exercise often helps the high adrenal type burn off the excess adrenaline. Those with low adrenal function should usually not exercise until the body regains its footing through nutritional and diet support. When the body's reserve is increased, a gradual scaling up of isometric and isotonic exercises can be considered.

Step 3: Determine the Severity

Adrenal Fatigue Syndrome in its mild form is clinically very different from its more advanced stages. Symptoms of mild and early stage AFS may include insomnia, lack of energy, irritability, high blood pressure, salt craving, anxiety, and weight gain. Additional symptoms of advanced Adrenal Fatigue Syndrome, however, can include hypoglycemia, *low* blood pressure, heart palpitations, weight loss, severe depression, and menstrual irregularities. Using the same recovery tools that were successful for mild AFS to treat those in more advanced stages might backfire. In other words, the right tools for early stage AFS can lead to worsening symptoms in those with advanced AFS. Misunderstanding this principle is a common mistake.

We use the tools to reach our goals, and choose the tools based on our underlying strategic concept. Without this clear conceptual strategy that guides how and when to use the tools, they easily can be misused and produce undesirable results. Evaluating and knowing each sufferer's clinical state helps us choose the tools to use, but we also understand that no single tool works all the time. As the body changes, the choice of tools must also change. Clearly, what is nutritionally beneficial for one person may be toxic for another. However, what was beneficial for a person at a particular stage could be negative for that same person during the course of recovery.

Step 4: Prioritize and Personalize

We prioritize and time our nutritional therapeutic recommendations to match the body's readiness. Most people in advanced AFS have many problems involving other organ systems. By prioritizing our approach, we can systematically create a plan while not losing sight of what is important at any point in time. For example, some with both ovarian and adrenal dysregulation improve fastest and do best if we deal with the ovarian dysfunction first. The opposite may apply for others. Still, for some, we need to approach both simultaneously.

We facilitate sustained recovery by taking a one-step-at-a-time approach. We prefer a gradual and enjoyable steady path to recovery rather than one dominated by periods of euphoria followed by setbacks. Such a pattern can worsen the overall condition and slow down the entire recovery process.

Step 5: Challenge the Body

In order to give the body the most gentle and valuable nutrients possible, we use qualitative nutritional challenges, which are specific protocols we follow in order to prove or disprove the underlying hypothesis. A challenge helps us gain insight into the body's response before we choose the tools from the recovery toolbox. For example, we can gain insight into the body's aldosterone regulation by drinking salt water and seeing how the body reacts. It's essential that we understand the purpose of each challenge, and both positive as well as negative responses provide valuable information. Well planned challenges in various forms help us to understand the body's readiness before embarking on a nutritional therapeutic course.

Step 6: Monitor Closely

We carefully monitor the body's reactions by using a listening-focused, narrative approach with close follow up. This means we listen to what is being reported to us. Currently, we don't have objective and quantitative tests to assess adrenal function in real time. Our Total Body Approach calls for taking small steps, and we constantly evaluate and update, getting as close to real-time body reaction as possible. We do this by paying attention to the various signs and symptoms the body exhibits every day. We are especially attentive to how a body performs under challenges and how it reacts under stress.

For many centuries, medical practices used this listening-focused, narrative-based approach—it was the norm. However, it's now an endangered art form because modern clinical medicine relies heavily on investigative tools. Certainly, astute health practitioners use the many investigative tools at their disposal, but final recommendations are usually based on an extensive patient history, clinical insight, and experience. This is even more important with AFS because we lack complete understanding, and laboratory results are not very reliable.

Step 7: Patience

Biological repair takes time. The body isn't like a light switch that we turn on and off at will. Our use of gentle nutrients facilitates internal, sustainable, and long-term change at the cellular level. Many do show signs of improvement within a reasonable period of time, but severe cases can take much longer.

Bear in mind that proper adrenal recoveries usually take a series of steps resembling going up a flight of stairs, with lots of pauses in between each step. The first few steps up are usually fast, with short pauses. By the end of this stage, most are overjoyed as they rediscover and reclaim their lost energy. While the total energy state of the body is still far below that of someone whose health is optimal, most AFS sufferers are happy to have the energy for a balanced social, work, and family life. As we progress further up the recovery stairway, pauses become longer, and the incremental increases in energy become fewer. This is normal. With proper planning, a steady and sustained recovery can usually be achieved, provided we have patience and allow the body to rest when called for.

If no improvement is noted for a sustained period of time, we often find a very good, but hidden, reason. No amount of water can put out a fire if oil is quietly added on the side. Those in this category need patience in order to initiate a systematic approach to discovering the underlying cause. Most of the time, if we look deep enough we can find the hidden reason. Those who focus on understanding the body will likely find it, and in our role as clinicians we facilitate that process. We usually have to say goodbye to those who are too focused on quick recovery or are unrealistic in their recovery goals. Granted, it's relatively easy to stimulate the body and drive energy output. However, that approach eventually backfires and AFS worsens because the root cause is never uncovered and dealt with.

If we look at recovery as a race to the finish line in a track meet, our Total Body Approach is akin to running at a steady pace and feeling fresh at the end line. It's about enjoying the race along the way, rather than sprinting, only to collapse well before the finish line.

Many with AFS tend to have Type A personalities, defined as intense, compulsive, and always inquisitive. They often want to understand the science of AFS, which can be beneficial. However, we discourage patients from *excessive* focus on trying to explain every single symptom or physiological pathway, because this tends to increase anxiety and further drains the body of its already limited reserves. Overall, it slows recovery. We find that those who recover completely at a relatively fast pace trust and listen to our recommendations and follow them carefully. We encourage everyone to use their energy doing what they enjoy in life in a balanced way, stopping to smell the flowers along the way.

Being Mindful of Limitations

Our Total Body Approach can facilitate, but not mandate what the body does. We can affect recovery only as fast as the body allows a long term, sustained return to health. Some do well in a short time; with others, the preparation period may be longer. Those who are older or constitutionally weaker often face the biggest challenges. Therefore, we remain constantly on the lookout and open to alternative methodology.

The Big Picture

Our Total Body Approach integrates the best of conventional and natural healing processes nutritionally. Our focus is deploying natural compounds to satisfy what the body is crying out for, and we believe in accommodating the body's requests whenever possible. We teach those who seek our help to listen to the body, which is something many of us do not know how to do.

Given the right tools, the body is capable of bringing about its own healing, at least in most cases. We are facilitators of this process. In addition, our Total Body Approach calls for a focus on the whole person by integrating a holistic approach. Along with recovery, our goal is to teach each person how to live post-recovery, and how to prevent recurrence in the future. Finally, to give the body ample time to recover, patience is a hallmark of our approach. We do not force the body into functions for which it is not prepared.

Key Points to Remember

- The AFS recovery tool box contains many tools. Knowing what to use and when, are signs of clinical excellence.
- Our Total Body Approach comes after years of helping those with AFS recover. It is a comprehensive and nutritionally oriented program designed to give the adrenal glands the right gentle tools for it to self-heal instead of forcing it to perform with stimulants.
- The approach is formulated based on four basic foundational principals and contains seven specific steps.

Chapter 8

Looking to the Future

Now that you have read *Adrenal Fatigue Syndrome*, we hope you see, as we have, that it is part of the body's complex neuroendocrine stress response that merits our attention. While the adrenal glands may be at the forefront of attention in terms of symptomatology, the broader picture points to a continuum of systematic activation at first and eventual dysregulation of our neuroendocrine stress response system when pushed to the limit. *The autonomic nervous system is also dysregulated in addition to the adrenal glands in advance stages. The entire continuum is best termed Stress-induced Neuroendocrine Syndrome* (SINS). Therefore, full attention needs to be paid to the entire neuroendocrine system if we are to get to the bottom of this condition physiologically. At the deeper mental level, it reflects our body's inability to handle the complexity of modern life and the body's wise desire to return to simplicity for survival. No organ system is spared as the body forces us to deal with survival in the most rudimentary terms.

Currently, most conventionally trained doctors simply are not educated about AFS in medical school and postgraduate training. The quest in scientific medicine for complete understanding through modern scientific methods has advantages and could even be considered noble. However, a lack of complete understanding of a condition should never stand in the way of using natural therapies that achieve consistent and reproducible, positive, clinical results—and without negative consequences.

Intellectual arrogance has no place in the healing arts and can lead to a loss of practical wisdom. In order to truly understand Adrenal Fatigue Syndrome, we first need to humbly commit to filling in the gaps in our knowledge of neuroendocrinology. Educating ourselves is the first step toward healing. This is our biggest task. That is why we present with great detail the science behind this condition—to dispel any myth that this condition is not real. If you are a sufferer, no one can tell you your fatigue is not real when you are bedridden. Your body does not lie. As far as AFS sufferers are concerned, all they want is to get better. Although we have tried to explain the physiology and psychology involved in AFS, we know that most sufferers are less concerned about every pathological and physiological pathway than they are about therapies that will help them restore their health.

For clinicians, a lack of understanding can never negate positive clinical results, especially when patient evidence-based results are overwhelmingly positive. Fortunately, more forward looking health practitioners are now taking this seriously.

Common sense needs to prevail. We are at the crest of an information explosion on the neuroendocrine basis of how our body handles stress and its clinical ramification, Adrenal Fatigue Syndrome. This book is part of that movement, as we endeavor to educate the world about this condition. By now, you know why we have chosen to become part of this movement to educate and help. *Too many women and men are afflicted and have nowhere to turn.*

We have described the experience of many sufferers, and they enter choppy waters indeed. Their well meaning efforts at self care and healing often seem so logical at first, but end up detrimental in the long run. They deserve better.

The tide toward a more holistic approach in medicine is well on its way. Consider:

- 90 percent of Americans believe in natural medicine, and 70 percent have tried some form of alternative medicine sometime in their life.
- 40 percent report that vitamins and herbs are first choice therapies. Massage followed at 29 percent as the second most common therapy, followed by aromatherapy, yoga, and homeopathic products.
- About 74 percent of women and 57 percent of men take vitamins on a daily basis.
- 69 percent reported having used alternative medicine during the past year.
- In total, the number of visits to natural medicine health practitioners exceeds the number of visits to traditional MDs.

You are not alone if you feel helpless and lost in your quest to better health. Like many of our colleagues, we also are western trained and educated. We consider ourselves privileged to have discovered Adrenal Fatigue Syndrome and to have taken it seriously, because we believe in two vital principles:

- First, the body never lies;
- Second, just because something isn't within our body of knowledge, doesn't mean it does not exist.

In fact, our lack of knowledge was exactly what propelled us to pursue information about this complex condition over the years.

This book reflects, then, the product of our academic knowledge and clinical experience with Adrenal Fatigue Syndrome in the real world. We need much more research to more completely understand AFS in it social, physiological, and psychological context. We are excited and grateful to be in the forefront of clinical neuroendocrinological and AFS research and pass on our findings and experience to those who suffer from this condition and to our colleagues in healthcare who want to learn more. In the end, knowledge is the best prescription for healing, but our knowledge of the body and its workings are still far from complete. The more we know, the more we know how much we don't know. For example, with close to a century of research, we have yet to find a cure for the common cold or prevent hypertension at its root. We hope this book has given you a comprehensive view of the clinical profile of Adrenal Fatigue Syndrome, from its many physical, mind-body, and constitutional components. It is a complicated condition, and we make no apologies for saying so.

Our hope is that you are encouraged by knowing that recovery is at hand if you embark on a proper and comprehensive recovery program. We know recovery is possible because many have done so under our guidance. We also pledge to help you stay current on this dynamic, exciting field. The most effective way to stay current is through our website,*www.DrLam.com.*

Sign up for our free newsletter and watch for news and updates as more research comes online.

Thank you for joining us on this journey.

Michael Lam, M.D., M.P.H.
Dorine Lam, R.D., M.S., M.P.H.

Appendix A

Finding the Right Practitioner

The right healthcare practitioner can change your life. In the case of Adrenal Fatigue Syndrome, this is usually the most critical piece of the puzzle. Why? Because the vast majority of those with AFS experience myriad convoluted symptoms that confuse all but the most astute clinicians trained in this condition. It's essential to know what each symptom means, along with its significance. As you can see from the case studies, the right professional guidance can mean the difference between successful recovery and persistent failure.

Due to the general lack of Adrenal Fatigue Syndrome expertise among conventional and even alternative health practitioners, finding the right practitioner is easier said than done. Those with advanced Adrenal Fatigue Syndrome face the greatest challenges, as many have already been abandoned by conventional medicine and left to self-navigate.

It's worth spending the time to find the right clinician. Generally speaking, he or she should be an open minded and nutritionally oriented health professional. Additional clinical experience in endocrinology, cardiology, psychiatry, and neurology is beneficial, along with knowledge of using natural compounds in a holistic setting.

Insist on someone who can individualize your care, and look for someone who can examine diagnostic tests but also see beyond them to discern how you feel. Seek the clinician who believes that managing your adrenals requires a comprehensive approach, including modifying your diet, lifestyle, and exercise; this person's approach to natural compounds is both gentle and systematic and non-stimulating. Remember that a wrong approach can worsen your condition over time. In today's managed care and specialized environment, this is not an easy task, but neither is it impossible.

The Doctor Interview

You are entitled to ask a doctor key questions before making an initial appointment, and then based on the answers, ask yourself if this person is receptive to new ideas. What is his or her philosophy on how stress can affect the body? This will give you clues as to whether this doctor is holistic or conventional.

Later, when you talk with this doctor, does he or she clearly communicate the reasons you feel the way you do? An experienced doctor will generally have little problem tying in your various symptoms and giving you a comprehensive explanation. You should be able to receive direct answers to your questions in a way you can understand. This is part of being patient-oriented.

You can also ask about the doctor's philosophy of the adrenal glands as a key to the body's overall well-being and your symptoms of fatigue, along with other organ systems associated with your complaints, during the investigation. These questions help you indirectly gauge not only the doctor's knowledge of the adrenal system, but the more subtle understanding of adrenal function and Adrenal Fatigue Syndrome.

How to Best Communicate With Your Doctor

A good relationship is a two-way street, so the more clearly you communicate your problems, the easier it is for the doctor to address the issues. Here are simple tips to facilitate good communication:

- Have confidence in yourself, but do not show either an overly aggressive or passive attitude.
- Keep a journal of your health-related events and symptoms, noting when they come on (time of day or relating to an event or the menstrual cycle, for example), how they affect you, how you feel, and how and when you recover.
- Write down questions ahead of your appointment, so you can ask good questions and make the most of your appointment time.
- Trust your instincts. Your body is always right. Persist in finding the care you deserve. Don't settle for less.

Although we realize many doctors do not welcome patient-generated research, and some even become annoyed when patients bring them information, we recommend that you help your doctor stay informed. Print out articles relevant to your condition that you believe may help your doctor understand your situation, and submit these to your doctor for perusal ahead of time. Our Adrenal Fatigue Center at *www.DrLam.com* contains numerous articles that we constantly update. You can direct your doctor to our website. Forward thinking doctors, the real visionaries, thank us for providing this information online so they can learn and better serve their patients.

You have also benefitted from this book and other articles. You can better explain and describe your symptoms when you know more about your body and various conditions. This in turn helps your doctor help you.

If your doctor does not understand or cannot explain to you what is happening with clear confidence, chances are you need to consider finding another healthcare professional.

Investigate Other Options

Here are several tips if you cannot find the right practitioner:

- Connect with others who've had similar symptoms and investigate what they did to overcome their dysfunction. Do be careful not to draw conclusions too quickly, however. What works for one person may not work for another. You may be able to find a doctor through those who have been helped.
- Use the Internet. Search Adrenal Fatigue Syndrome and study relevant sites. Focus on educational sites that offer scientifically based information. Our site *www.DrLam.com* is a public educational website that contains the most easily searchable complete library of material on Adrenal Fatigue Syndrome on the web. Many articles on Adrenal Fatigue Syndrome not present in this book are available online, along with the latest news, FAQs (frequently asked questions), and an archive of questions many have asked through the years. You'll also find video and audio presentations of lectures on Adrenal Fatigue Syndrome. Those who like to be kept up to date on the latest news on this topic can sign up for our free electronic newsletter.
- Be wary of Internet forums because views expressed are often skewed and not objective in nature. What works for one person can in fact be toxic for another. Be skeptical of anyone who purports to have simple, quick fix or break-through solutions. Watch out for those who post angry

messages or who are overly active online. These individuals may have hidden agendas or unresolved psychological or undisclosed physical issues well beyond AFS. Finally, be careful of one-size-fits-all approaches; these seldom work except for the mildest cases.

- If you are not sure whether you have Adrenal Fatigue Syndrome, or if you would like an assessment on the degree of your adrenal function, take our Three Minute Test in this book (Appendix F) or online at *www.DrLam.com.*
- If you have specific questions about your symptoms or condition, write to us directly from our website at *www.DrLam.com.* Each question is individually answered privately and in confidence.

Fortunately, travelling is not usually required in order to seek help. We serve clients all over the world. If you cannot find a practitioner with whom you are comfortable, or if you have no one to turn to, call us. (For details see our website.)

Our telephone-based nutritional coaching program is an individualized one-on-one program designed to facilitate the fastest possible recovery using natural measures. It incorporates many principles and techniques discussed in this book.

Appendix B

Seven Adrenal Recovery Mistakes

By this time, you know that most cases of Adrenal Fatigue Syndrome are mild (Stages 1 and 2), lasting a few days or weeks, with eventual full recovery. This generally occurs without awareness that AFS is involved. A minority of people find recovery a challenge. Their symptoms last longer than usual; they eventually improve, but never fully recover. Still, a smaller number of people slowly decompensate and their condition gets worse with time. These are the individuals who slowly slip into advanced stages of AFS (Stage 3 and beyond).

When sufferers experience frequent episodes of Adrenal Fatigue Syndrome symptoms that increase in severity and duration, we consider this a sign of recovery failure. The body has a built in, self repair system, but it is often not fully engaged in the recovery process. We see many reasons for this failure, and we discuss seven of the most common below. Keep these in mind as you embark on your search for help.

Mistake 1: Following Advice from Inexperienced Healthcare Providers

As they embark on a journey of recovery, most patients quickly realize that most mainstream physicians are not well educated about AFS. On top of this, modern medicine has a tendency to lean heavily toward laboratory-based approaches to healing, rather than narrative, body-based approaches. In addition, we do not yet have accurate and foolproof laboratory testing for Adrenal Fatigue Syndrome. *Paradoxically, the more advanced the adrenal weakness, the lower the clinical correlation with laboratory results.*

To untrained physicians, the maze of complaints is a challenge. Dysfunctional adrenals affect virtually every system of the body including the central nervous system, cardiovascular system, peripheral nervous system, hormonal system, and gastric system, just to mention a few. Therefore, practitioners need a thorough understanding of neurology, cardiology, endocrinology, and psychiatry. Since most physicians specialize today, their training is on a narrow, clinical focus, and they often lack experience in the multiple disciplines necessary to fully comprehend AFS in its broadest sense.

Unfortunately, treating symptoms becomes the standard of care instead of focusing on the root problem. This is why patients often end up with myriad prescriptions, including antidepressants and antianxiety medications, along with other agents that treat symptoms. Many different specialists often treat sufferers separately for digestive disorders, gynecologic disorders, psychological symptoms, allergies, and so forth.

The number of physicians with true expertise in advanced Adrenal Fatigue Syndrome invariably gained their expertise from years of clinical experience. In severe cases, full recovery can easily take a year or more. Inexperienced practitioners are often misled by laboratory tests and preoccupied with treating symptoms. These practitioners find it difficult to handle other than the most mild and straightforward cases of AFS and usually give up when it comes to advanced cases. Unfortunately, sufferers are unaware of these limitations and are misled into thinking they're on the right track. Disappointed, they eventually self-navigate as their symptoms get worse. Finding the right healthcare professional is your greatest challenge and task. Appendix A offers some tips on how to find the right physician for you.

Mistake 2: Excessive Use of Prescription Drugs and Medications

We live in a world where *symptoms are often classified as diseases*. Therefore, controlling symptoms is often confused with "curing" the disease, even when the condition is chronic. In the case of AFS, this common approach frequently ends in disaster. Masking pain, for example, is not the same as curing the condition that causes the pain. The symptoms of AFS are like pain, they're signals that something is amiss. But suppressing symptoms doesn't work and only punishes the body. The body responds by punishing with worsening symptoms.

The logical approach is to give the body the tools to heal itself, while monitoring the symptoms and using them as a barometer to evaluate progress toward healing. Sadly, this method is rarely deployed. Suppressing symptoms with various prescription medications is the norm. Unfortunately, most medications have side effects. For example, the dozens of common side effects of antidepressants alone include dry mouth, blurred vision, constipation, sleep disruption, headaches, nausea, loss of libido, and agitation. We can multiply this by the number of medications many individuals take simultaneously. Needless to say, this practice stresses the liver and the adrenals, and many with Adrenal Fatigue Syndrome never fully recover when their treatments are based on prescription medications, which can range from steroids to antianxiety drugs to sleep medications.

Mistake 3: Over Reliance on Laboratory Testing

As we learned in Chapter 1, *Diagnostic Tests—What You Need to Know*, diagnostic testing is severely limited when it comes to Adrenal Fatigue Syndrome. It is common to have significant AFS symptoms, but the lab tests are within the normal range. We often see lab results that confuse and mislead. Laboratory interpretation is challenging even for experienced clinicians. Physicians often find themselves chasing a moving target. In advanced AFS, the more we rely on laboratory tests, the more confused we get because of multiple inconsistencies in the correlation between test results and symptoms. As a result, patients are often subjected to numerous trial and error protocols undertaken by physicians with the best intentions but who were clinically misled by laboratory tests. This approach further weakens the body's already low adrenal function. Many come to us confused and frustrated as a result.

The body's signs and symptoms are far superior in gauging adrenal weakness than laboratory test results performed with current technology. The gold standard remains a good and comprehensive narrative history of the sufferer taken by an experienced clinician. Laboratory tests can be helpful when properly used.

Mistake 4: Improper Use of Nutritional Supplements

You likely know that natural compounds differ from prescription drugs in many ways. Prescription drugs usually follow a well defined and highly predictable efficacy curve, meaning that the desired response is usually generated within a predetermined range of therapeutic dosing. The body does not have a natural, built-in system of metabolizing non-natural compounds such as synthetic drugs, so with high dosages, toxicity results. Similarly, when natural compounds are used inappropriately, recovery is not only impeded, but the condition worsens over time. In these situations the compounds do more harm than good. This is one of the greatest mistakes made among those who embark on self-guided and nonprofessionally guided programs, especially if the Adrenal Fatigue Syndrome is advanced. (See Chapter 19, *Nutritional Supplements for Nutritional Fatigue: An Introduction* in the main book *Adrenal Fatigue Syndrome: Reclaim Your Energy and Vitality with Clinically Proven Natural Programs.*) for more detailed information about the use of natural compounds.)

Mistake 5: Failure to Recognize Paradoxical and Unusual Reactions

When medical treatments, usually with a drug, have the opposite effect of what we expect, we call that a paradoxical reaction. For example, if a sleep medication causes worsening insomnia, we call it a paradoxical reaction. Likewise, if a sedative causes hyperactivity, that's a paradoxical reaction. We see this when steroid drugs worsen AFS instead of helping. Experienced clinicians watch for these abnormalities.

Although we don't know the reason, paradoxical reactions are generally more prevalent with natural compounds. We do know that one person's beneficial natural compound can be toxic to another person. This can occur over time. In some cases, however, the body rejects these nutrients from the beginning. Instead of feeling better with an energy boost, the person feels worse and an adrenal crash could result.

The more advanced the AFS, the more paradoxical and unusual reactions tend to surface. The body is caught in a cascading downward state, with exaggerated responses mediated by hormonal imbalances in a positive feedback loop platform, along with its own violent attempt to rebalance itself. Such paradoxical reactions include:

- Severe fatigue but feeling wired at the same time.
- Fragile blood pressure that fails to normalize in quiet times.
- Reactive hypoglycemia despite metabolic medications to stabilize blood sugar.
- Palpitations made worse with cardiac medication designed to reduce irregular heart beat.
- Sudden anxiety attacks while on sedatives.
- Worsening fatigue with natural compounds that helped before.

While some of these symptoms can be due to drug intolerance, liver clearance problems, autonomic nervous system dysregulation, and side effects of natural compounds, many paradoxical reactions occur with no apparent medical logic. However, these paradoxical reactions are important warning signs of our body we need to take heed of. Failure to recognize such reactions can contribute to delayed or failed recovery.

Mistake 6: Failure to Recognize Multi-organ Involvement

Failure to recognize the multi-organ involvement associated with Adrenal Fatigue Syndrome often leads to a narrow focus that makes the condition worse off over time. As previously explained, the adrenal glands are regulated through the hypothalamic-pituitary-adrenal (HPA) axis. The adrenals themselves are then intricately connected to many other organs in a variety of axes. In women, one such intricate relationship is called the ovarian adrenal and thyroid (OAT) axis (Chapter 8, *Stage 3B—Hormonal Axis Imbalances* of the main book *Adrenal Fatigue Syndrome: Reclaim Your Energy and Vitality with Clinically Proven Natural Programs*). These three organs are intimately codependent on each other for optimal function. In men, the adrenal and thyroid are connected.

In the case of the OAT axis, when a medication alters one of the organs' functions, it will invariably lead to an often unrecognized change in the other two organs. For example, if thyroid medication is administered, it is not uncommon to see concurrent menstrual irregularities, a function of the ovarian hormones, and reduced ability to deal with stress and worsening fatigue, a function of the adrenals.

When multiple organs are involved and decompensate concurrently, the body's ability to recover is made much harder. For example, processing and assimilating nutrients becomes compromised, leading to reduced absorption of nutrients in the GI track, producing digestive symptoms. Liver function is reduced, although laboratory test results might be in the normal range. If not processed and metabolized properly, good nutrients become toxic, producing toxic metabolites that circulate in the body. If not properly cleared, these toxic metabolites can lead to brain fog, joint pain, skin rashes, allergies, muscle discomfort, and multiple chemical sensitivities among many other symptoms.

When the adrenals are not in optimal condition, no organ system is spared dysfunction. Therefore, an adrenal recovery program that does not factor in other organ involvement invariably fails as the condition worsens.

Mistake 7: Lack of a Comprehensive Recovery Program

The body is a closed ecosystem with a built in capability to self repair. If given a chance, it normally can recover on its own with the proper nutrients, lifestyle, dietary changes, and time. Recovery strategies focusing on this comprehensive approach often produce excellent results, even in severe cases, in a short time. By contrast, strategies that focus on controlling the symptoms and getting quick results often fail. For maximum recovery speed, the root cause, such as removal of stressors, improper dietary habits, and improper use of nutritional supplements, needs to be addressed through a comprehensive program.

The most effective recovery program should incorporate the following (which we discuss in detail later in this book):

- A customized nutritional supplementation program based on the person's internal needs and sensitivities.
- A customized dietary program based on the sufferer's metabolic needs.
- A customized lifestyle program including exercise based on the person's constitution and energy reserve.

The above three-pronged approach can produce dramatic and quick results if carried out under the supervision of an experienced clinician.

By now you realize that AFS is much more complicated and debilitating than you might have thought. Fortunately, with an individualized recovery plan, most patients can and do recover.

Key Points to Remember

The 7 most common recovery mistakes are:

- Following advice from an inexperienced healthcare provider.
- Excessive use of prescription drugs and medications.
- Over reliance on laboratory testing.
- Improper use of nutritional supplements.
- Failure to recognize paradoxical reactions.
- Failure to recognize multi-organ involvement.
- Lack of a comprehensive recovery program.

Appendix C

Tips for Special Occasions and Travel

As you now understand, recovering from Adrenal Fatigue Syndrome requires self care and vigilance. Recovery (and crash prevention) also requires adjusting your daily lifestyle to minimize stress and allow for adequate rest. However, you may need or want to travel and enjoy special occasions, too. We included this chapter to help you manage a variety of events and offer pre-crash management tips.

Special Events

Weddings, holidays, birthday parties, commemorations, and gatherings of all kinds are stressful for many people, regardless of their health status. Family conflicts and other personal issues tend to surface, schedules become crammed with events, and for some, travel looms. We've all seen pictures of travelers stranded in airports because of delays. Seldom do holiday seasons progress smoothly and without stress.

Obviously, for those with Adrenal Fatigue Syndrome special occasions and holidays can be an ordeal beyond the typical hustle and bustle of that time of year. For many, Christmas/Hanukkah shopping or days of wedding planning, for example, are presented as fun and rewarding, but they can be extremely stressful activities. Without realizing it, we change our breathing patterns during stressful times and events, causing the body to go into a sympathetic overtone. If you have AFS, it is imperative that you do your Adrenal Breathing Exercises at various times during your daily activities:

- Before you leave the house.
- During the car/bus/train ride to the store.
- While walking through the aisles.
- During snack/meal breaks.
- After you have returned home.

Other Tips for Special Occasions

- If possible, celebrate holidays (any of the major holidays in your country) or other special events away from home. This avoids the additional stress of concerning yourself with all that goes into getting ready for company.
  If you feel up to it, bring a dish along for the holiday meal. However, listen to your body. If you don't feel up to cooking, don't push yourself—you have alternatives and choices. Plan to go out for a birthday dinner or if possible have food for a wedding or baby shower catered. Overwork can trigger an unwanted adrenal crash.

- Plan in advance. Rushing around at the last minute causes adrenaline to start flowing, which in turn can increase your anxiety level, which is certainly not conducive to enjoying yourself.

- If you are traveling any distance and might be away more than a day, bring sufficient supplements to cover last minute delays and change of plans.

- Everything is ramped up during busy holiday and common vacation weeks: airports are not only busy, but chaotic; parking lots are packed; and all kinds of transactions, from airport check-in to finding restaurants on the road seem to take longer than expected. That's why we recommend that you travel with snacks in your glove box, handbag, or briefcase, so you can keep your energy level up no matter what life throws your way.
- Snack regularly and bring snack foods with you, even when you're headed to a meal at someone else's house or are heading to a restaurant. Your meals are often delayed, and if you encounter crowded restaurants, everything slows down from ordering to delivery.
- Care should be taken to avoid any formula that contains alcohol as a preservative, due to its potential negative effects on the liver.
- Strictly watch your sugar intake! With Adrenal Fatigue Syndrome, the body is highly sensitive to sugar, and unfortunately, sugary foods are extra plentiful during parties and holiday celebrations of all kinds.
- Try to maintain a normal sleep schedule and do your best to avoid staying up too late. If you're tired, find a way to take a short nap to recover the energy spent.

Air Travel Tips

At one time, most people considered air travel quite manageable. In recent years, however, even the hardy among us have had to adjust to changing conditions, including increased security, frequently cancelled flights/fewer flights, and increased costs and decreased services. While most people adjust, those with Adrenal Fatigue Syndrome dread the grueling experience of air travel. The weaker the adrenals, the higher the chance that air travel can trigger an adrenal crash. The following tips serve to prepare you for departure and ensure you arrive in the best shape possible:

Pre-Travel Tips:

- If possible, plan to travel with a companion, a person willing to be the runner, so to speak, able to take care of your needs during the trip and handle most of the check-in process and the baggage.
- Try to schedule your travel during your best and freshest time of the day. Avoid red-eye flights because they disrupt your circadian cycle.
- To the extent possible, avoid layovers, but if you must stop, try to schedule a long layover of 48 to 72 hours, thereby allowing the body time to adjust.
- If there is a weight limit imposed by the airline, weigh your luggage at home to avoid last minute surprises.
- To conserve energy, do not engage in strenuous exercise on the day before and the day of departure.
- Take an additional recommended booster dose of your supplement prior to departure.
- Print out the boarding pass ahead of time with the seat assignment on it.
- Choose a rolling carryon bag and keep it as light as possible—avoid a backpack as a carryon bag—but do

take a neck pillow or regular pillow, as well as lumbar support for the plane ride.

- Pre-pack at a leisurely pace, starting a few days prior to your departure date, and remember to include prepackaged snacks in your carryon baggage. Check your travel documents and store them in your carryon baggage.
- To minimize stress, arrive at the airport well ahead of schedule. Have your travel companion or cab driver drop you off at the terminal doors.
- If possible, confirm your seat assignment to avoid being bumped. For convenient access to restrooms and to minimize walking, ask for an aisle seat toward the front of the plane.
- Many international airports provide short term beds and showers at reasonable prices within the terminal. If necessary, take advantage of these services.

At the Check-in Counter:

- Luggage is best checked at curbside; if that's impossible, seek help from a porter to get to the check-in counter or wait for your companion. Do not lift any heavy baggage by yourself.
- Once inside the terminal, find a place to sit down, using your upright luggage if necessary. Do not stand in line unless no alternative exists. Again, wait for your travel companion to handle the check-in for you. Try to stand as little as possible.

- Ask for the "meet and assist" wheelchair/cart service (usually provided free of charge) from the check-in counter to the gate, especially if the walk to and from the gate is long.
- Carry an empty water bottle with you to bring past the security checkpoint, unopened snacks, and extra supplements accessible at any time, along with your books and music devices and headphones. The idea is to go through security with ease.

From Security Check Point to Gate:

- This is often the most chaotic area within the airport and has the most potential to drain your energy. We often forget that the brain is bombarded by the noise and x-ray emissions. It's also stressful to follow the many instructions for passing through security, i.e., taking off your shoes, belts, jewelry, hats, and so forth.
- If you can, preserve your energy by sitting on your carryon baggage if the line is long. Lean against your companion as needed, but don't force yourself to stand for long periods. Do your Adrenal Breathing Exercises whenever possible.
- Once you've passed through security, sit down if you are tired and do the Adrenal Breathing Exercises. Go to the restroom where you can sit and do these exercises.
- Ask your travel companion to fill your water bottle, and as a precautionary measure, drink some water and eat a snack—even if you don't feel like you need it.

- Take your time and rest for a few minutes before continuing to the gate.
- Unless you're traveling alone, ask your companion to guide you to the correct gate, so that you don't need to look up and search for it. Do not stop to window shop along the way.
- Walk slowly—you've allowed extra time, so you aren't pressured to rush. Use the escalators or moving sidewalks, terminal trains or busses, or golf cart service to conserve energy. Sit when you can and ask for help with your carryon bag.

At the Departure Gate:

- Sit in the least congested place in the departure lounge. Ideally, stay as far away as possible from computer monitors, TV screens, and loud music, and as close as you can to a water fountain and restroom.
- Stay relaxed with quiet reading or listening to personal music. Don't chitchat unless you have to—unnecessary talking will drain your energy.
- Purchase a meal to bring with you on the plane so your scheduled mealtimes are disrupted as little as possible.
- Go to the bathroom immediately before the boarding phase.
- Do Adrenal Breathing Exercises as often as needed.
- If you are not using a wheelchair service, be the last to board, so you don't have to stand in a long line. By the time you board, others will have cleared the aisles.

On the Plane:

- If you have luggage for the overhead compartment, ask your companion to stow it for you, and if you're traveling alone, ask the flight attendants for help.
- Avoid watching action oriented TV or any videos. Enjoy music instead.
- Put down the window shade to avoid bright sunlight and/or use eye shades to block light and visual stimulation.
- Stand up, stretch, and walk to the restroom as needed, but avoid standing in the restroom line for a prolonged period of time.
- Drink fluids frequently—the air is very dry inside the plane. Ask for water as needed.
- If your current seat is noisy because of passenger conversation and activity, ask if a seat change is possible.
- If meal service is included, ask the flight attendants not to wake you if you are sleeping, but do ask that your meal be saved for a later time; however, don't depend on the airline for the proper food. Always bring your own.
- If you have a tendency to be hypoglycemic, it's especially important to have plenty of snacks with you, so you can eat according to your body's schedule, not the airline's.
- If you anticipate being tired upon arrival, ask the cabin crew to prearrange wheelchair/ cart service on arrival.
- Fill in arrival forms ahead of landing.
- Do Adrenal Breathing Exercises frequently.

On Arrival:

- Unless you are seated in the front of the plane, let others exit first and take your time.
- Ask for help retrieving your overhead baggage.
- If it's a long walk to the baggage claim, drink water and eat a snack, even if you don't feel as if you need it.
- Don't stop to shop.
- It is normal to be excited when you arrive at your destination, but try to remain calm and serene throughout this last leg of your trip.
- At the baggage claim, let your travel companion take over. If you're traveling alone, always ask for help.
- Once you've arrived, take a nap—consider it mandatory. Then you will feel up to other activities.

We wish you safe and healthy travels!

Key Points to Remember

- Special events are an unavoidable part of balanced living.
- Learning to plan ahead will greatly reduce any chances of crashing and help you enjoy the occasion.
- Air travel is one the most common triggers of adrenal crashes. Fortunately, this too can be managed calmly and systematically.

Appendix D

Your Adrenal Recovery Journal

As you recover from Adrenal Fatigue Syndrome, we recommend keeping a journal, which encourages you to keep good notes about your symptoms and progress. Keeping a journal promotes a state of mind that focuses on details and keeps your memory fresh so that you don't forget recommendations.

Journaling also allows you to reflect on what you're doing right and perhaps figure out how to improve when you believe you are falling short on carrying out your plan. This allows you to track any immediate adjustments before too much time has lapsed and the damage is done. We also recommend recording questions you may have for your doctor or recovery coach.

Over time, your journal will serve as an authentic self-navigational tool that will help you to recover from Adrenal Fatigue Syndrome. The only equipment you need is a notebook and a pen. Include the following things in your journal:

Your Supplement Instructions: Record the times you are advised to take your supplements each day and the quantity.

Fatigue Scores: Fatigue scores record two important parameters of your energy state each day. It is comprised of two components. First, the amount of resting time you need each day in order to have the energy to perform your regular chores. Second, the percent of normal daily activities you can do.

For example, if you *needed* a 30 minute nap to get through the day smoothly (whether or not you were actually able to take a nap), your score is 0.5. If you were capable of doing or did 70 percent of your normal daily activities, such as performing your job or business, or carrying out a normal load of errands, your score is 70. Similarly, if you were capable of or performed 90 percent of your normal household chores without feeling tired, your score is 90. Your entries for these categories would look like 0.5/90. Tracking this fatigue score over time will give you an objective measurement of your progress.

Optional Categories

- *Food intake*, as well as restrictions and adjustments.
- *Exercise regimen*, paying special attention to how you feel before and after exercise, specifically, how much energy you have after exercising.
- *Sexual activities*, and if you feel drained afterwards.
- *Hypoglycemic episodes*, frequency, intensity, and the time between episodes.
- *Bowel movements*, the patterns, especially if there is constipation, loose stool, or diarrhea.
- *Sleep patterns*, describing the problem, as in going to sleep (sleep onset insomnia or SOI) or waking up and being unable to go back to sleep (sleep maintenance insomnia or SMI). The sleep aids you took and your use of other sleep supports. Write down your sleeping and waking times. Since sleep often is especially challenging, consistent recording will help you spot a trend.

- *Emotional states* such as anxiety, depression, jittery, anger, or irritability.
- *Menstrual cycle*, tracking the dates and duration of your cycles along with symptoms. This is particularly important for those who tend to crash during their menses.

If any one of these areas is of particular concern, begin tracking it on a scale of 1-10, with 10 as the worst, 5 being average, and 1 being the best. For example, if you have had no hypoglycemic episodes today, the score is 1. The importance of these numerical parameters will be evident to you over time. However, do not track more than 3-5 categories at any one time. Trying to assess too many issues all at once can be stressful and overwhelming. You can always add categories to track later.

To begin, we recommend focusing on the key category of fatigue. Energy levels reflect most other underlying root issues in Adrenal Fatigue Syndrome. When the fatigue and energy levels improve, many of the underlying symptoms, such as sleep and anxiety, will have automatically improved as well.

It's a good idea to do all the scoring and recording at the end of the day, putting the relevant scores on the bottom of each day's entry. Briefly note what transpired that day, and if you experienced any changes.

Avoid Over-Journaling

If you don't have anything special to put in your journal and you have no overall change, skip that day and wait for the next. The key is to record significant events that alter the scores, most commonly, an adrenal crash—or the lack of a crash. Also note other negative life events, i.e., loss of a loved one, an infection, troubles on the job or in your business, problems arising with family, and so forth. The presence or absence of a crash or symptoms provides information on your adrenal reserve and the body's ability to withstand stress.

When there is significant change in any of the scores, take some time to reflect on the reasons and write them down. Your journal should be informative and act as a memory trigger. However, we don't want journaling to become a stressful activity. Most of the time, it takes no more than 5-10 minutes a day. Remember, too, that the information is for your personal use only.

Key Points to Remember

- Keeping a simple personal journal is an important recovery tool.
- It serves as an authentic self-navigation tool in the future.
- Important entries include supplement schedule, the fatigue score, and overall well-being.
- Do not over-journal, as it can drain you of precious energy.

Appendix E

Suggested Reading and Resources on the Adrenal Fatigue Syndrome

In addition to the books, CDs and DVDs listed in the front of *Adrenal Fatigue Syndrome*, here are additional free readings and resources from our website, *www.DrLam.com/afs/*. When on the site, just click on the topic of interest. Each will help you understand the scientific basis of our approach to Adrenal Fatigue Syndrome we take throughout this book.

Acidosis
Aging Brain
Andropause
Atrial Fibrillation
Beef, Chicken, or Fish
Blood Thinners and Nutritional Supplements
Chelation
Cholesterol
Dehydration
Detoxification
DHEA
Diabetes
Eggs—Good for your body?
Endometriosis
Nutritional Supplements—To Take or Not?
Omega 3 Fatty Acid
Oral Health
Progesterone
The Big Fat Lie
Estrogen Dominance
Fibroids
Heart Disease Prevention—A Complete Nutritional Approach
Hypothyroidism
Insulin and Aging:
Magnesium and Aging
Menopause
Metabolic Syndrome
Milk—The Perfect Food?
My Doctor Is Killing Me
New Markers of Cardiovascular Disease
Nutritional Medicine
Upper Limits Vitamin C and E Intake
Water
Where to Buy Supplements
Why Conventional Medicine Rejects Adrenal Fatigue Syndrome

After Recovery

After your recovery from Adrenal Fatigue Syndrome, the natural progression is to embark on an anti-aging program where you begin to reverse the biological clock naturally, while keeping AFS at bay. We have a complete library on this in our website. The following articles are helpful and found also on *www.DrLam.com/afs/.*

Anti-aging Program	Dr. Lam's Smoothie Recipe
Anti-aging Strategies	Customized Exercise Routine
Blood Type Diet	Links to Various Health Centers
Osteoporosis	Calories That Count
Woman's Optimal Daily Allowance	Men's Optimal Daily Allowance

Links to Natural Protocols for Common Health Conditions

For the Avid Reader in Natural Health

You can download our free online ebooks from our home page at *www.DrLam.com:*

Beating Cancer with Natural Medicine
5 Proven Secrets to Longevity

Other Useful Links

New information and links on natural health and Adrenal Fatigue Syndrome are regularly added to our website library. These include many nonprofit educational organizations, links to scientific journals, periodicals, and additional recommended books.

Here is the link: *http://www.DrLam.com/links.asp*

Appendix F

3 Minute Adrenal Fatigue Syndrome Test

Here is a checklist of common symptoms associated with Adrenal Fatigue Syndrome. Check the boxes that are applicable. See your score below and find out what you can do about it.

- ☐ Tendency to gain weight especially at the waist and inability to lose it.
- ☐ High frequency of getting the flu and other respiratory diseases that tend to last longer than usual.
- ☐ Reduced sex drive.
- ☐ Lightheaded when rising from a supine position.
- ☐ Unable to remember things and unclear thinking.
- ☐ Lack of energy in the mornings and also in the afternoon between 3-5:00 PM.
- ☐ Feel better suddenly for a brief period after a meal.
- ☐ Need coffee or stimulants to get going in the morning.
- ☐ Crave for salty, fatty, and high protein food such as meat and cheese.

- ❑ Increased symptoms of PMS for women; periods are heavy and then stop, or almost stop on the 4th day, only to start to flow again on the 5th or 6th day.
- ❑ Pain in the upper back or neck for no apparent reasons.
- ❑ Easily startled.
- ❑ Decreased ability to handle stress and responsibilities.
- ❑ Body temperature is off balance; hands and feet feel cold, face feels warm, or hot flashes.
- ❑ Unexplained hair loss.
- ❑ Tendency to tremble when under pressure.
- ❑ Multiple allergies such as asthma, hay fever, skin rashes, eczema, hives, and food sensitivity.

Enter the number of checkmarks you have made: ______

What does your score mean?

If your score is 4 or below, chances are you do not have Adrenal Fatigue Syndrome unless your symptoms are quite severe. There may be other dysfunction in place. Adrenal Fatigue Syndrome is unlikely to be significantly involved, although we can't be sure without a detailed history. You can adopt many of the dietary and lifestyle recommendations in this book as they are generally conducive to good health. Group 1 and 2 nutritional supplementations (Chapters 20 and 21 in the book, *Adrenal*

Fatigue Syndrome) are generally well tolerated if your doctor approves. If you do not improve within a reasonable amount of time, write to us through our website with your score and what you did. We will give you our thoughts in confidence.

If your score is 5-9, you may or may not have Adrenal Fatigue Syndrome. Many conditions mimic AFS, so if you have not already done so, visit your doctor for further medical investigation. If you are given a clean bill of health but remain symptomatic, consider Adrenal Fatigue Syndrome. The higher your score on the test, the higher your risk of Adrenal Fatigue Syndrome. You also can adopt many of the dietary and lifestyle recommendations mentioned in this book, but be cautious when it comes to nutritional supplementation, as they can worsen the condition if not properly used. If you are not sure where you stand or what to do, then write directly and privately to us online through our website (*www.DrLam.com*) with your score and a brief history. We'll give you our assessment and suggestions in confidence.

If your score is 10 or above, it is imperative that you become fully educated about Adrenal Fatigue Syndrome and alert your doctor about this condition. The more severe your symptoms, the more dysfunctional your adrenal glands likely are. We *do not* recommend self-navigation as it often makes the condition worse over time. If you cannot find someone knowledgeable to help you, if you fail to improve on your recovery plan, and are not sure where you stand or what to do next, then write to us directly and privately through our website (*www.DrLam.com*). Let us know your score, a detailed medical history, and your main complaints. We will reply to you in confidence and give you some guidance.

This free test is also available online at our website *www.DrLam.com.*

About the Authors

Michael Lam, M.D., M.P.H., A.B.A.A.M., is a western trained physician specializing in nutritional and anti-aging medicine. Dr. Lam received his Bachelor of Science degree from Oregon State University, and his Doctor of Medicine degree from the Loma Linda University School of Medicine in California. He also holds a Master's degree in Public Health. He is board certified by the American Board of Anti-Aging Medicine where he has also served as a board examiner. Dr. Lam is a pioneer in using nontoxic, natural compounds to promote the healing of many age-related degenerative conditions. He utilizes optimum blends of nutritional supplementation that manipulate food, vitamins, natural hormones, herbs, enzymes, and minerals into specific protocols to rejuvenate cellular function.

Dr. Lam was first to coin the term, *ovarian-adrenal-thyroid (OAT)* hormone axis, and to describe its imbalances. He was first to scientifically tie in Adrenal Fatigue Syndrome (AFS) as part of the overall neuroendocrine stress response continuum of the body. He systematized the clinical significance and coined the various phases of Adrenal Exhaustion. He has written four books: *The Five Proven Secrets to Longevity, Beating Cancer with Natural Medicine, How to Stay Young and Live Longer, and Estrogen Dominance.*

In 2001, Dr. Lam established *www.DrLam.com* as a free, educational website on evidence-based alternative medicine for the public and for health professionals. It featured the world's most comprehensive library on AFS. Provided free as a public service, he has answered countless questions through the website on alternative health and AFS. His personal, telephone-based nutritional coaching services have enabled many around the world to regain control of their health using natural therapies.

Dorine Lam, R.D., M.S., M.P.H., is a registered dietitian and holistic clinical nutritionist specializing in Adrenal Fatigue Syndrome and natural hormonal balancing. She received her Bachelor of Science degree in Dietetics, holds a Master's Degree in Public Health in Nutrition, and a Master of Science degree in Nutrition from Loma Linda University, in Loma Linda, California. She is also a board-certified, Anti-Aging Health Practitioner by the American Academy of Anti-Aging Medicine. She coauthored with Michael Lam, M.D., the book *Estrogen Dominance* and numerous articles on Adrenal Fatigue Syndrome. Her personal research and writing focuses on the metabolic aspect of Adrenal Fatigue Syndrome.

She is married to Michael Lam and is an integral part of the telephone-based nutritional coaching team helping people overcome Adrenal Fatigue Syndrome.

Printed in Great Britain
by Amazon